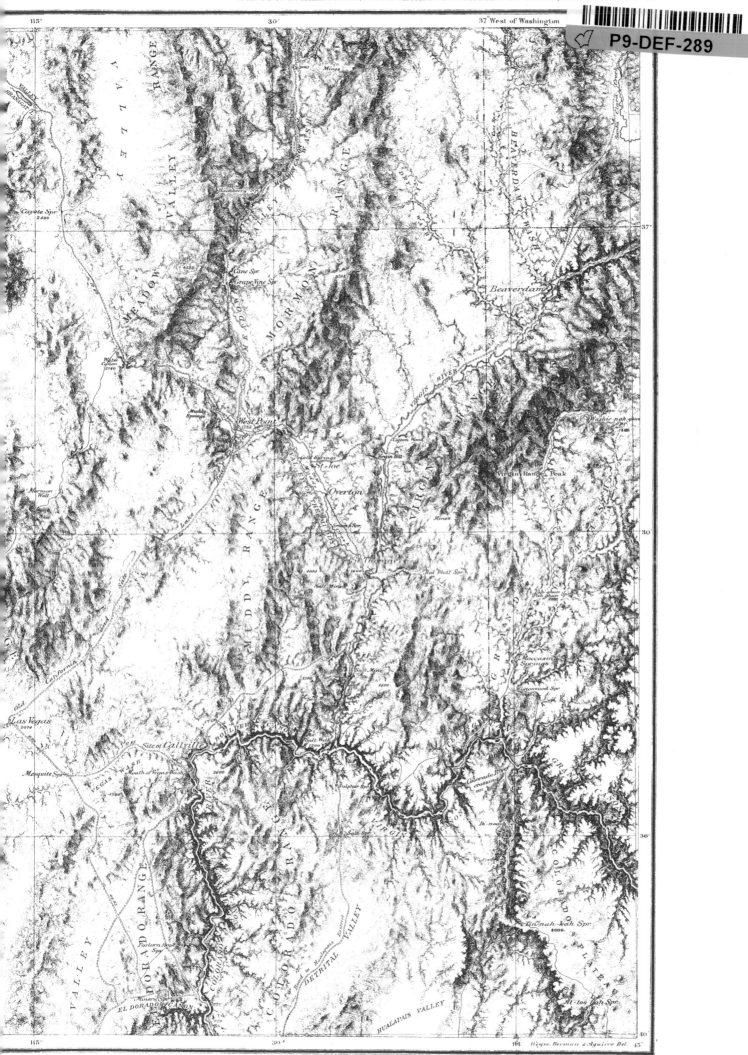

1st. Lieut. Geo. M. Wheeler, Corps of Engineers.

Las Vegas

Las Vegas

As it began—as it grew

by Stanley W. Paher

maps and illustrations by Roy E. Purcell

NEVADA PUBLICATIONS
Box 15444
Las Vegas, Nevada

Front Cover: "Las Vegas, Block 16, 1905"
A hand-colored etching by Roy E. Purcell

Printed in United States of America

Library of Congress Number 70-175114

Nevada Publications
Box 15444
Las Vegas, Nevada 89114

Table of Contents

Dedicated to Florence Lee Cahlan

Preface

The City of Las Vegas was founded on May 15, 1905.

It was a hot dry day. In the dazzling mid-morning sunshine, under a veil of canvas stretched above a wooden stand, mustached officials of the San Pedro, Los Angeles & Salt Lake Railroad Company auctioned townsite lots before a crowd of more than a thousand.

Railroad planners had selected this site on the dreary sagebrush desert in the midst of Las Vegas Valley because of its location about halfway between Los Angeles and Salt Lake City at a point where water was abundant.

A day or so after the auction, one newcomer had only criticism for the burgeoning town. "Las Vegas is unquestionably one of the dustiest places in all creation," he said while gazing at the countless mules and horses in long-line teams continually moving in and out of town. Mingling with these were dozens of two-horse teams drawing local delivery wagons with merchandise and supplies.

As the heavy wheels of each rig cut deeply into the ungraded streets, puffs of powdery dirt arose to form an umbrella of dust over the town. Some of it settled into the wagon ruts to be churned by other wagons and teams, but most of it drifted onto tent and wooden houses and filtered through the cracks of walls.

Every brisk storm was an endurance test. Rampaging desert winds flattened plank houses and bulldozed flimsy canvas shelters. Las Vegas also seemed to be in the path of every wandering dust-devil madly twisting across the valley. Annoyed by hours of dust-laden fitful gusts, a Los Angeles *Times* reporter wiped his notebook and scribbled, "To be happy in Las Vegas, one should not try to stay clean."

Though the town was new back in 1905, Las Vegas already had a varied history which dated to 1831 or 1832 when the first annual Mexican trading caravan passed through here from New Mexico on the Old Spanish Trail. From Santa Fe, hand-woven blankets were transported in the fall of each year to Los Angeles where they were traded for California mules and cattle. That colorful era lasted until 1848.

Beginning in 1855 the Mormons maintained a religious mission and outpost at this strategic point linking its settlements in Utah with San Bernardino, California and the Pacific Ocean. They cleared land for cultivation, grew crops, built a fort and mined lead in the nearby mountains. Several factors led to abandonment of the settlement in 1858.

In the early 1860's various individuals tried to rebuild what the Mormons had left behind, but not until Octavius D. Gass and others who came in 1865 did anyone succeed in renewing the farm. The resulting Las Vegas Ranch flourished for the rest of the century and proved to be the area's first enduring settlement.

Early twentieth century railroad building in southern Nevada drastically altered the area's economic make-up. The founding of Las Vegas in May 1905 was the most dramatic change. The town grew fast as a trading center and distribution point for area mines. In 1908-09 much political maneuvering brought about county seat status for Las Vegas.

After 1910 the story is better known. Las Vegas remained distinctly a railroad town until about 1930, when Hoover Dam construction sparked the first major boom at Las Vegas. Fifty-percent increase in population resulted within five years. As late as 1940 the official census for Las Vegas listed only 8,422 residents.

Early in the 1940's another boom followed. It was brought about by the establishment of the Las Vegas Aerial Gunnery School (later renamed Nellis Air Force Base), the creation of the nearby town of Henderson where defense and industrial plants arose, and the construction of additional resort hotels along what soon became the famed Las Vegas Strip.

Though the end of the 1940 decade passed quietly, the beginning of atomic testing at the Nevada Test Site northwest of Las Vegas and the continued expansion of resort facilities resulted in spectacular growth in Las Vegas through the 1950's. Additional hotel building in the decade of 1960 and in the early 1970's helped bring about the internationally known city of today.

With each decade an era closed and a new one began. In each a crisis developed and hundreds of "smart people" forsook Las Vegas because the economy was supposed to be in its death throes without visible future prospects. But in every growth period there were faithful, courageous people who invested in the area's future in a variety of enterprises.

Back in 1905 when Las Vegas was in the midst of a rugged patch of desert, those earliest settlers had to be tough customers to get along. Long-time residents who were present at the town auction and stayed to develop the town were: W. R. Thomas, John S. Park, C. P. "Pop" Squires, Ed Von Tobel, Sr., John F. Miller, Edmund W. Griffith, J. T. Mc-Williams, Ed W. and Frank A. Clark, W. C. Thomas, W. E. Hawkins, Henry Squires, Walter R. Bracken, Dr. Roy W. Martin, Adam and John Kramer, Peter Buol, J. S. Wisner, Dan Noland and Jake Beckley.

These and other intensely loyal men boosted Las Vegas at every opportunity. They gave of themselves in return for the blessings bestowed upon them. They devoted hours to civic projects, battling for street improvements, water systems, lighting, and laws and ordinances to provide shelter and security for growing families.

Existing literature about Las Vegas other than surface impressions is almost non-existent; writers have done little serious research in depth. Blinded by the flashing neon, latter-day critics have repeated the same falsehoods about Las Vegas and left distorted impressions about the town and its people. Sunday magazine supplements and nationally circulated magazine articles have persisted in referring to Las Vegas as an "Electric Sodom" or a "Modern Gomorrah," describing the nightlife as "unabashed opulence" exemplified by a "garish quagmire of lacquered ladies."

Even the few books published about modern Las Vegas are almost wholly devoted to the entertainment and the night life, with the gossip of gamblers and bartenders undoubtedly serving as prime source material. Their provacative titles have magnified the same tabloid sensationalism: "City of Sin," "Great Fraud," "Green Felt Jungle," and "Zoomtown."

These writers have overlooked the obvious—that behind the glamor the Las Vegas story essentially reads like that of any progressive American city. Its developers overcame hardships, just as those did who founded Chicago and Sacramento and Phoenix. They endured the wind, dust, and flies, and heat that often soared to more than 115 degrees. The absence of air conditioning compounded these inconveniences. In all directions were vast expanses of sand, alkali, and scrubby desert growth.

Gradually these were subdued. Mesquite and sagebrush were uprooted to make way for gardens. Flies were less numerous after internal combustion had replaced the hayburners on the thoroughfares. Thousands of cottonwoods, elms, umbrella, ash, and fruit trees were planted to provide wind breaks and shade, thus making the town cooler. Lawn planting and street paving held the dirt and dust in place. Swamp coolers and finally modern air conditioning tamed the desert heat.

The present volume tells the beginnings and early growth of this rich story behind the city. Modern development and the personalities who made it possible await their day in another book. Among towns throughout the world of approximately 250,000 Las Vegas may well be the youngest because its birthdate was at the start of this century —1905. Probably no other *metropolis* in the world could boast of a resident populace who can remember when their town was founded. That fact alone makes one stop and ponder about the magic growth of Las Vegas!

Good reading,

August, 1971   Stanley W. Paher

Acknowledgments

While researching and compiling this history of early Las Vegas, I received much encouragement and the generous cooperation of several individuals and institutions.

Florence Lee Jones Cahlan gave extraordinary assistance to this book especially in two ways: she patiently edited the entire manuscript and offered numerous valuable suggestions concerning the substance of both the text and picture captions. In specific instances she rescued me from ignorance by furnishing data from her files. Since she was employed as a general reporter and feature writer with the Las Vegas *Review-Journal* from 1933 until 1953, her personal observations gave me insights into local developments.

Roy E. Purcell's art, displayed in the artwork in the early chapters, shows a deep respect for Southwestern history and for the desert. The six maps in this volume come from his creative pen. He also helped in the design of this book, in addition to offering valuable comment on the text.

K. C. Den Dooven crystallized hopeful thinking by suggesting that I enlarge to book length an existing small manuscript on Las Vegas. To this project he brought his enthusiasm and as time permitted his publishing skill, guiding the manuscript through a maze of technicalities.

The courteous staffs at the Las Vegas City Library, University of Nevada at Las Vegas, and the California State Library made research pleasant. Nevadans Pete Cole at Panaca and Maryellen Sadovich and Californians Dock Marston of Berkeley and David F. Myrick of San Francisco all answered queries.

Fenton M. Gass, son of Las Vegas Ranch founder Octavius D. Gass, freely related invaluable childhood reminiscences of ranch life in Las Vegas Valley around 1880. His older sister, Lelah Vegas Gass Slaughter, also was interviewed. Both died in December 1970 at ages 96 and 97 respectively.

Indefatigable researcher Dennis Casebier provided useful references and offered suggestions which helped shape the chapters on Fort Baker and Las Vegas Ranch. Bob Griffith's wealth of Las Vegas experiences provided information and data for captioning many pictures. Captain Ray Gibson provided stories about Las Vegas in its infancy.

Mrs. Theron Fox, Glenn Butterfield, Sherwin "Scoop" Garside and Ralph Roske all made valuable editorial suggestions, as did some of Las Vegas' prettiest young girls—Ann Knouft, Joan Shelton, Patti Liance, Leslie Payne, Jean Greer and Georgia Lewis. Helen Holland and Harriet Gray transcribed tape recordings, and Norma Grahame prepared the copy for typesetting.

Pictorial assistance came from a number of individuals who generously loaned their albums and collections to this project. Five collections deserve special mention—those belonging to Sherwin "Scoop" Garside, Mrs. Maureen H. Wilson, Special Collections of the University of Nevada Las Vegas Library, the Ed Von Tobel Lumber Company and the Stay family of Las Vegas. Less extensive but equally valuable help came from individuals listed in the picture credits listed in the back of this book. Las Vegas photographer Frank Mitrani processed many of the pictures used.

To everyone I tender my sincere thanks.

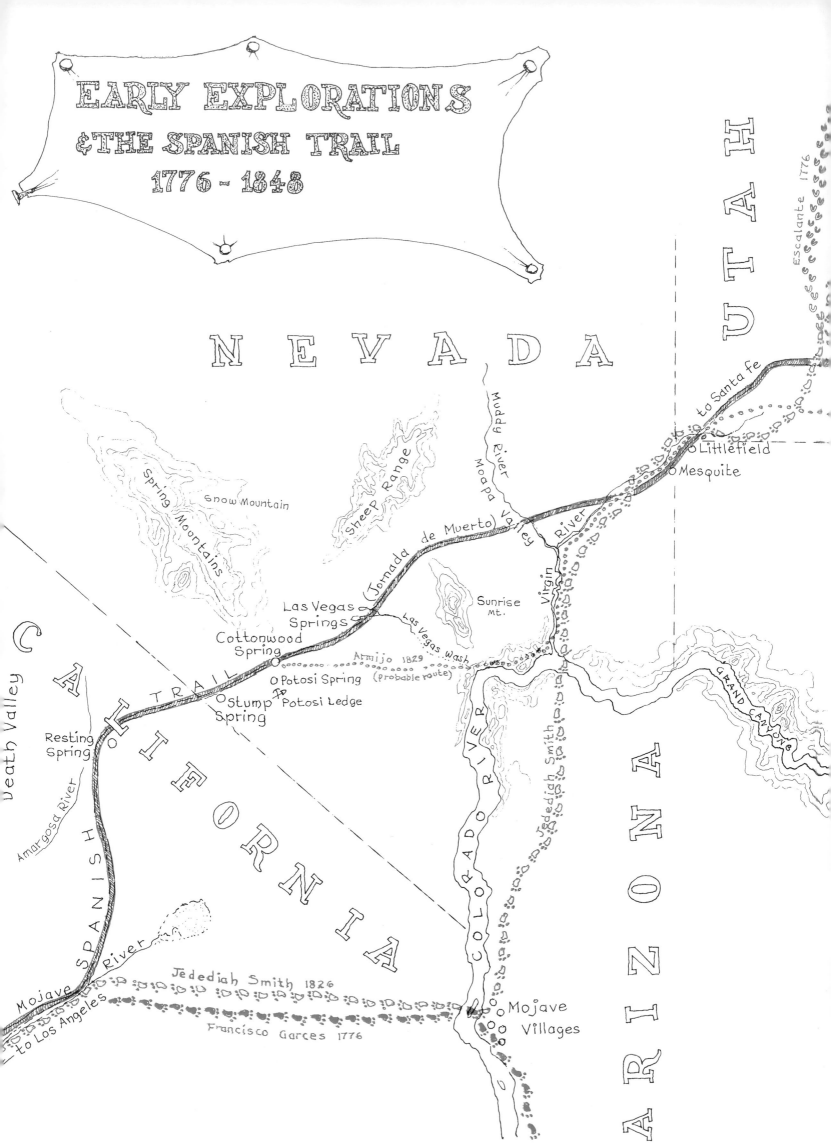

CHAPTER ONE

Old Spanish Trail Days
at Las Vegas

IT WAS A HOT DAY IN THE FALL OF 1832. A THIN DUST cloud dug up by hoofs of a few score horses and mules rose above the purple mountains northeast of Las Vegas Valley. The warm desert sun beat down from almost overhead, and only a few lazy clouds blemished the blue autumn sky. An extended pack train of Spanish and Mexican traders hastened to the springs at Las Vegas—The Meadows—a long green belt of mesquite trees in the midst of this brush-covered valley. The traders regarded Las Vegas as one of the most welcome sights along the entire length of the Spanish Trail.

Most of the time The Meadows lay undisturbed, and hot dry winds and dust-devils swirled across the valley and against the brink of a low hill, where a deep swift current tumbled and flowed from a series of bubbling springs eastward into Las Vegas Wash. Paiutes living in the nearby Spring Mountains and nomadic Indians from the Colorado River often sampled this water and shade, but they moved on unless there was a reason to stay. On this day there was.

As the dust cloud moved closer to The Meadows, the near-naked aborigines crouched in sand hills near the springs, awaiting opportunities to kill stray animals from the intruder's camp.

Soon the cloud began to break up and the caravan revealed itself. Unburdened stock guided by their innate sense of smell bolted for the water. Close behind, as fast as their burdens would permit, heavy-laden pack mules, tongues lolling and mouths grunting with each step, pressed onward to the precious life-stream. No longer did the furiously swearing horsemen need to crack their whips to sting their animals into action.

The long train halted where the loose stock were drinking. Each mule brayed impatiently to be relieved of its pack, but the stock had already started to turn away from the water to nibble the tender green blades along the banks. After the muleteers loosened the ropes and removed the packsaddle carrying two to four hundred pounds of various types of hand-woven woolen goods such as *fresadas, colchos, serapes* and *tirutas,* the animal broke into a run to bury his mouth in the water. The men arranged packsaddles and packs in a little corral and covered them with matting for protection against rain. A small trench which the men dug drained away any sudden torrent. The corral also formed part of a barricade.

With each day's stop the muleteers rotated meal preparation. While a few men searched among the mesquite trees for campfire fuel, another untied ropes from a mule carrying the *metate*—a stone block upon which maize was ground to make tortillas. Soon everyone but a few posted guards responded to the smell of frijoles, chile colorado and coffee to renew themselves before taking a siesta. The difficult Muddy River-Las Vegas drive had been completed by traveling at night and early morning to avoid the sun's hot rays. For several hours they rested under a relay of guards, while the stock continued to gorge in The Meadows.

After a day or so the caravan prepared to strike out southwest for Cottonwood Spring and eventually into California. With the animals fed and well watered, the muleteers reloaded the equipment. A hand-softened raw sheepskin which prevented chafing was placed on the animal's back. Next came a saddlecloth and then finally a stuffed leather saddle which lay as flaps on the mule's back. A broad grass band which secured the saddle was drawn so tightly that the animal grunted and groaned; but when the load was snug the mule traveled comfortably.

The heavy packsaddle was placed on top as if it were a single pack. Stronger mules carried two packs of equal weight, one on each side, balanced and coupled together by a rope. A stout rope was then thrown over all, drawn tightly under the belly and laced around the packs. For protection against the rain and the incessant dust, a square piece of matting enveloped the bundle.

Two men could pack a mule in three minutes. A leather blinker temporarily placed over the animal's eyes kept him quiet. The packer had an assistant who adjusted and tied the ropes. When they were taut he shouted "adios!". The packer, after rejoining with "vaya!", made fast the rope on top of the packsaddle, and sang out "anda!". The mule trotted away to join the others in munching grass until all mules of the caravan were packed.

After further preparations the caravan headed toward Cottonwood Spring. For 18 autumns after about 1831 or 1832, the pack trains left Santa Fe and other New Mexico points to trade woolen goods at settlements up and down the Pacific coast for strong California mules and stock. In the following spring the traders regrouped east of Los Angeles for the long journey home. Eastward caravans had droves numbering from a few hundred to more than three thousand animals. On the return trip all caravans refreshed themselves with the Vegas' cool waters.

No one knows who first disturbed the tranquility of the springs. Though Indian eyes first glimpsed The Meadows in the unknown past, whites came much later because the vast sage and sandy wastes stretching in every direction from Las Vegas Valley discouraged investigation. Initial exploration of peripheral areas is credited to Francisco Garces, a hardy Friar and renowned pathfinder of the New Mexico-Southern California trail via the Gila River in southern Arizona. He ventured northward in 1776 from the present Yuma area along the Colorado River into the Mojave Indian country on the east side of the river. Once arriving at a point near modern Needles, the Garces party swung west toward Los Angeles by way of the Mojave River. While legend has it that Garces glimpsed Las Vegas Valley, evidence in his journal shows that he did not even enter Nevada. He missed its southern tip by five to ten miles.

The same year that Garces explored the deserts along the Colorado River, Francisco Escalante's party of about eight men left the New Mexico capital, Santa Fe, on horseback, intending to reach Monterey and the California coast by way of what is now Utah. While moving through Utah's fertile central valleys, Escalante pioneered portions of the Spanish Trail, but he, too, failed to enter Nevada. The approach of winter and a lack of provisions forced him to turn back and the padres recrossed the Colorado River at a point which became known as the Crossing of the Fathers. Neither Escalante nor Garces established a route between the adobe settlements of New Mexico and California's coastal missions as hoped, and not until exactly a half century later did anyone further explore the interior Southwestern deserts.

When the Republic of Mexico won independence from Spain in 1821, the new government encouraged friendly commercial relations, including a fur trade, between the modern California and New Mexico areas, then both under Mexican control. In 1826 the great American trailblazer, Jedediah Smith, left his trapping areas along the Utah-Idaho border to search for new beaver country and the mythical Buenaventura River. Smith headed southward for the California coast and followed portions of Escalante's route in south-central Utah before blazing a new trail southwest along the Virgin River. While following that river out of Utah, Smith intersected the Nevada border in November 1826 at a point near the modern community of Mesquite in eastern Clark County, eighty miles east of Las Vegas. He was the first American to enter modern Nevada, though to British fur trader Peter Ogden goes the honor of first Caucasian in Nevada. He entered northern Elko County in June 1826.

Smith eventually crossed the Colorado River at nearly the same place that Garces did five decades earlier and then followed the earlier-found route along the Mojave River, eventually reaching Los Angeles. This exploratory trip, repeated late in 1827, helped establish portions of the Spanish Trail in southern Utah and eastern California.

Others soon followed the imperfect route of the Spanish Trail which Smith tied together. The Ewing Young-Kit Carson party of 1829 traversed the western end of the Trail, from a point east of modern Barstow into the Los Angeles Basin. That same year the notorious "Pegleg" Smith reportedly journeyed along a portion of the Trail from the Virgin River in southwestern Utah into Los Angeles essentially tracing the steps of Jedediah Smith. The evidence for this is fragmentary. In the fall of 1829 after obtaining Jed Smith's counsel, Peter Ogden and his party left the Northwest to trap beaver in streams tributary to the Colorado River. Ogden also proceeded along portions of the Trail in Utah.

Antonio Armijo's sixty-man party which journeyed from the village of Albiquiu, New Mexico on November 7, 1829, to Los Angeles made important deviations on the known· route after leaving southwestern Utah. With a large supply of *serapes* and *fresadas* to trade for California mules, horses and stock, Armijo followed Escalante's steps through northern Arizona past the Crossing of the Fathers and then intercepted Jedediah Smith's trail along the Virgin River. Following that stream as it flowed toward the Colorado River, the caravan re-entered Arizona near its northwest corner, halting on Christmas Day 1829 near the site of Littlefield, Arizona.

From there a reconnaissance party rode ahead southwest in the direction of the Mojave River to seek watering places along a possible short cut. If springs were found, the party could avoid the longer and more dangerous trip taken by Jedediah Smith and others down the Colorado River into the rugged Mojave Indian country and thence westward over parched desert plains to the waters of the Mojave. The older segments formed unequal legs of a right triangle; if the unknown hypotenuse could be traversed, it would be about forty miles shorter.

With scouts sent ahead the main party continued into Nevada down the Virgin River. At its confluence with the Colorado River the advance group and the others reunited, except for Rafael Rivera, an experienced young scout who pushed on westward to the Mojave River, which he had seen only the year before. As the young rider moved west through unexplored desert lands, the caravan moved westward north of the Colorado River toward Las Vegas Wash. From there they would either proceed along the familiar Colorado River or with good news from Rivera they would blaze a short cut.

The daring horseman's route during his two weeks from the caravan was poorly recorded. After leaving the others at Virgin River he rode west and into Las Vegas Wash. At its upper end he glimpsed Las Vegas Valley. Sent to look for water holes, Rivera probably spotted the acres of verdant growth nurtured by Las Vegas Springs. If he stopped at the water he was the first white man to do so.

A NEW MEXICAN TRADER
(after Brewerton)

Pushing westward, he found Cottonwood Spring, the "Little Spring of the Turtle" at the present site of Blue Diamond, Nevada, as well as Stump Spring (in Pahrump Valley, Nevada) and Resting Spring (near Tecopa, California) before reaching the Amargosa and Mojave Rivers. Armijo recorded that Rivera found Indian villages on those rivers. The hardy scout rushed back with a favorable report and rejoined the pack train camped in Las Vegas Wash.

The caravan broke new ground as it moved westward out of the long ten-mile Las Vegas Wash, pitching night camps in a dry wash and beside a "dry lake" before reaching Cottonwood Spring the third night. While skirting Las Vegas Springs, the Armijo party was undoubtedly the first recorded group to enter the Valley. Las Vegas Springs were bypassed because Armijo said that he made two dry camps enroute Cottonwood Spring.

Early the next day the caravan continued its way over Mountain Springs Pass and a day later came to Stump Spring, two days away from the Amargosa River by way of Resting Spring. A few days later they reached the Mojave River which led toward Los Angeles, then a pueblo village containing fine gardens, vineyards and corn fields amid sparkling streams. The Armijo party disposed of their wares and rounded up precious stock for the return to New Mexico in the spring of 1830.

For the trip home the traders divided into three groups. One of these traveled the known route by which they came. After winding over the Spring Mountains and passing Cottonwood Spring, that party may have visited The Meadows instead of making dry camps as they had on the westward journey. No record of this exists, however.

Even without credit for discovering Las Vegas, Armijo's known contributions are of supreme importance: in leading the first commercial caravan to transport and exchange goods between New Mexico and California, he also opened up a highly desirable segment of the Spanish Trail, from Cottonwood Springs to the Mojave River.

A westbound party led by William Wolfskill and George Yount in September 1830 was the first to travel the Spanish Trail's entire length in generally its final form. (Armijo does not get that distinction because he did not use that part of the Trail as it arcs through western Colorado and central Utah; Armijo joined the Trail near the Utah-Nevada line.)

The Wolfskill-Yount party did not pioneer the route to Las Vegas; instead it moved down the Virgin and Colorado Rivers into the Mojave Indian country as Jedediah Smith had. It is not known which trading caravan first avoided any dependence of the Colorado River as a guide by traveling directly from the Virgin River to the Mojave River by way of the Muddy River and Las Vegas. The fifty-five thirsty miles of moistureless desert between the last two named points soon became known as the terrible *jornada de muerto*.

Whoever first traversed that short cut perfected the Spanish Trail. This probably happened in 1831 or 1832, only a year or two after Wolfskill-Yount. Thereafter each annual caravan, after plodding through the dry desert from the Muddy River, anticipated stopping at these life-saving springs. An early group named them Las Vegas—The Meadows—a sensible description of this oasis in the middle of the desert. The trade abruptly ended in 1848 when the United States took possession of this area after winning the Mexican War.

From its eastern terminus, the capital of New Mexico at Santa Fe, the Spanish Trail passed north of Arizona's Grand Canyon and through Paiute Indian country to reach "Vegas". The trail then crossed the Mojave desert, ascending Cajon Pass before dropping into Los Angeles, the western terminus. This trade route functioned from 1830 until 1848, when the United States acquired this territory. The Trail then gave way to easier and more direct east-west routes. When this map was published in 1849, Las Vegas was surrounded by vast stretches of uninviting land, though Americans had settled both to the northeast and west. Precipitous Colorado River canyons, burning deserts and high mountain ranges were barriers to exploration and settlement of southern Nevada.

Many Spanish Trail travelers described Las Vegas in their diaries, extolling the large lush meadow watered by a creek that rose from a series of four large springs. The united flow formed a swift, clear five-feet-wide and two-feet-deep current which ran east for several miles through the lowlands of Las Vegas Wash in the direction of the Colorado River.

Cottonwood- and willow-shaded grass which grew around the springs was adequate for the animals, though other satisfactory growth was about three to four miles east of the springs. Further below was a three-mile-wide by twelve-mile-long flat containing thousands of mesquite trees from which local Paiutes harvested beans as a principle part of their diet. A brief stay rejuvenated weary travelers and emigrants, but many remained several days to rest their exhausted animals.

The natural basins containing the springs were large enough to bathe in, and the lukewarm water gushed with such force that it buoyed a swimmer like a cork. The Mormon missionary George W. Bean wrote, "the water of the springs is very clear; they are from 20 to 30 feet in diameter, and at a depth of two feet the white sand bubbles all over as tho' it was the bottom, but upon wading in there is no foundation there. It has been sounded to a depth of 60 feet, without finding bottom; and a person cannot sink to the armpits on account of the strong upward rush of the water."

In the fall of 1848 Addison Pratt scribbled in his diary that the Vegas had the finest stream for its size he had ever seen. "The valley is extensive and...by the aid of irrigation [would] be highly productive. There is water enough in this rapid little stream to propel a grist mill...and oh! *such* water. It comes just at the termination of a 50 mile stretch without a drop of water or a spear of grass. Pah Eutahs here in great numbers, but they run from us like wild deer."

Las Vegas' best known visitor during the trade caravan era was John C. Fremont, who came on May 3, 1844. His cavalcade approached Las Vegas Valley from the west in regular formation. Scouts rode ahead and on the flanks of the main body consisting of front and rear divisions of well-armed Americans, Frenchmen and Germans, all in Spanish, American and Indian dress. About a hundred pack animals, baggage and horned cattle intermingled between the divisions. The party stretched for more than a quarter of a mile along the trail.

After traveling eighteen miles Fremont's band late that day made camp at Las Vegas, "two narrow

A "Digger" or Pah-Ute Indian
(after Brewerton)

15

streams of clear water, four or five feet deep [which] gush suddenly with a quick current, from two singularly large springs." At a water temperature of about 72°, the men found the pools refreshing for bathing. But the taste was too warm to be agreeable.

The next day Fremont's men started earlier than usual to face the longest dry march on the Trail—the *jornada de muerto*—which soon became noted for its somber toll exacted on travelers. In 1849, Pomeroy's emigrant train hourly passed the remains of mules, oxen, horses and all kinds of discarded property. When cattle gave out, compassionate men shot them rather then watch them perish.

S.N. Carvalho, Fremont's artist in his Fifth Expedition of 1854, noted that abandoned wagons, chairs, tables, bedsteads and other articles of housekeeping marked the trail southwest into Las Vegas. "It was not difficult to follow the trail; in one hour I counted the putrid carcasses of nineteen oxen, cows, mules and horses; what a lesson to those who travel over such a country, unadvised and unprepared." The suffering could have easily been imagined.

Besides emigrants, explorers and legitimate traders, many rustlers at intervals drove bands of horses and stolen California stock over the serpentine trail to New Mexico, deriving a quick profit from the hard drive. An Indian slave traffic also thrived. The wholesale robberies and connivance which occurred on the Trail shows what unrestrained and adventurous men these traders were. Their lawlessness cast disrepute on the entire business, often giving honest traders a bad reputation.

In an attempt to curtail any illegal traffic, authorities at Los Angeles imposed restrictions, especially in implementing price controls on animals and establishing assembly stations to inspect herds so that stolen animals might be recovered. Ultimately California officials secured the New Mexico governor's cooperation by requiring passports for all traders. A system of penalties was devised to punish lawbreakers.

After the trading era ended in the spring of 1848, the Mormons called that portion of the Trail from central Utah to Los Angeles the Southern Route to the Coast or, more simply, the Mormon Trail. Though the names were new, the route followed the familiar Spanish Trail. Soon this trail connecting the Mormons' Salt Lake City headquarters with Southern California came into more frequent use.

When many California-bound emigrants were in Salt Lake City in 1849, Jefferson Hunt, a leader of the Mormon Battalion and a hardy experienced trail guide, led a company of 107 wagons southward at a fee of ten dollars each. While many eventually withdrew from Hunt in favor of a route across Death Valley, he led the rest of the party through Las Vegas and into California.

Very late in 1849 renowned pathfinder Major Howard Egan camped at the springs for more than two days while traveling south from Provo, Utah. David Chessman's ox-team party in 1850 noted a lone unmarked grave and remarked that it seemed lonely and sad.

By late that same summer, the Mormon Trail had become so popular that Elijah Ward advertised in Salt Lake City's *Deseret News,* a guide service for travelers over the southern route to the California settlements. In an editorial the paper said that emigrants would do well to consider Ward's service. Though the road was good the editor had no doubt about Ward's ability to pilot anyone to Los Angeles from where travelers could move north to the gold fields on the Mother Lode. Ward collected a flat rate of ten dollars per wagon; an equal amount was also charged for each company of five footpackers or anyone with pack animals.

Beginning in December 1852 and each winter thereafter the Salt Lake-California mail began to be routed through Las Vegas and Los Angeles, instead of along the direct emigrant route which followed the Humboldt River in modern northern Nevada. The proprietor of the mails, George Chorpenning, was able to secure increased compensation because of the longer southern route.

In April 1854 Congress established a monthly mail route from Salt Lake City to San Diego, by way of uninhabited Las Vegas and the village of San Bernardino, California. The Mormons had founded that town in 1851 as part of a line of settlements between Salt Lake City and the Pacific Coast. Chorpenning again obtained the contract to deliver the monthly mail among these towns. His riders carried mail on horseback or on packmules, though they occasionally used wagons.

The same month that service began on the extended mail route, April 1854, Congress appropriated $25,000 toward construction of a military road from Salt Lake City to the eastern boundary of California. Late in December the *Deseret News* noted that the Mormon Trail would be followed with a few minor deviations. Though Las Vegas

On May 3, 1844, after journeying eighteen miles in a northeasterly direction from a point near Blue Diamond Springs, the expedition of John C. Fremont arrived at a very large basin "at ground called Las Vegas—a term which the Spaniards use to signify fertile or marshy plains." Fremont obviously did not give Las Vegas its name, as some have written. That small, wiry handsome soldier was barely thirty-one when he camped at Las Vegas Springs. His mustache led into a beard that extended the full length of his jaw.

Entering the foreground is an armed party of twenty-two men, in addition to animals and wagons. Because of their strange equipment and diversified dress, one man wrote that the party looked like it belonged to Asia rather than America. In the background is Red Rock Canyon and the Spring Mountains. Near the springs the men saw mesquite trees with their yellow flowers and a many colored assortment of spring wildflowers in bloom. Other species of shrubs were seen, and in his diary Fremont recorded their scientific names. No human inhabitants were to be found, although Paiutes often made temporary encampments at the springs that usually lasted through the winter.

17

was mentioned in the news story, it was not listed as a settlement.

Very early in 1854 a venerable western Nevada pioneer, John Reese of Mormon Station (Genoa) passed through Las Vegas. He had left Salt Lake City with twenty-four wagons of dry goods and groceries for the southern Utah settlements and then continued southward to San Bernardino, making the trip in just two months. At his destination he reported a theft of $9500 in gold which Brigham Young had commissioned to Reese for eventual delivery to the new San Francisco mint, scheduled to open in April 1854. On the return to Utah Reese carried a wagon load of newsprint for the *Deseret News*.

Reese's trip was a precursor to increased freighting traffic over the same route, which within two years saw numerous bullwhackers escorting trains loaded with foodstuffs and merchandise for Utah, all passing through Las Vegas. In April 1855 two San Bernardino traders sent several wagons with about 60,000 tons of merchandise to the Mormon capital.

Clearly, the Mormon Trail during the 1850's constituted the backbone of travel along the "Mormon Corridor" from Salt Lake City to San Bernardino. Missionaries, emigrants, mail riders and other travelers all stopped at the welcome springs of Las Vegas. Establishment of a permanent settlement at this popular campground was inevitable.

The site of these springs is on the south side of West Fremont Avenue, a half mile west of its intersection with Rancho Road.

LAS VEGAS SPRINGS

Chapter Two

Mission In Deseret

During the period from the fall of 1847 until the spring of 1855, the Mormons founded a score of important settlements in a direct line from Salt Lake City to Cedar City. They were connected by a good wagon road which only a year earlier had been improved beyond Utah through Las Vegas and the Southwestern deserts as far west as San Bernardino.

At the church's General Conference which convened at Salt Lake City on April 6, 1855, President Brigham Young announced among other things that he would colonize the heart of the desert between Cedar City and San Bernardino as part of southwest expansion of "Deseret". He selected Las Vegas then in part of New Mexico territory, as the settlement site because of an abundance of good water, rich soil and an agreeable climate. Church leaders had known of those advantages ever since the fall of 1847 when the Mormon guide Jefferson Hunt first passed through that oasis.

The settlement's main purpose was to establish a vital link in the "Mormon Corridor" which connected Salt Lake City and San Bernardino. Young listed other objectives of Las Vegas Mission after selecting William Bringhurst leader of the thirty-man party which would go there. He told the group to "go to Las Vegas, build a fort there to protect immigrants and the United States mail from the Indians and to teach them how to raise corn, wheat, squash and melons." In addition, the settlers were to extend the Mormon religion to the natives, thus helping to make the Southern Route to the Coast safe for travel.

In Mormon religious terms the method of ordering individuals to establish a new town or preach the Mormon gospel in a distant land was known as the "call system". It had two noble underlying principles: the church officers believed that they were divinely called to be leaders and, secondly, that there must be unquestioned obedience to their orders. This method successfully helped settle all of Utah beginning in September 1847. Devotion to that system was so disciplined that only two of the thirty men initially ordered to Las Vegas refused to make the trip.

In calling men for a mission, Governor Young always provided for a balanced company of agricultural workers and craftsmen. "We can make anything from a needle to an anchor, build a ship and sail it too," a Las Vegas missionary later boasted. Experienced men from older Utah communities were mixed with novices, who usually were recent arrivals from the East or European immigrants. Almost all colonies were thus quite successful. Only after crops were planted, living quarters built and peace established with the resident natives were women and children added to a colony.

On May 10, 1855 a party of Las Vegas-bound missionary-colonists left Salt Lake City after each man had sold sufficient possessions to buy a wagon load of provisions and had said goodbye to his family. After the southbound train had been on the road five days, mission leader Bringhurst's small party, which had departed later, overtook them. Organization of the mission then followed. First and Second Counselors were chosen and ten-men companies headed by a captain divided the group.

The uneventful trip to Las Vegas ended when most of the men reached the welcome Las Vegas

Springs in mid-afternoon on June 14, after they had driven thirty-two hours to cross the last fifty-five miles of waterless desert from the Muddy River. Others straggled in a day later with the help of the earliest arrivals, who had carried water back to them for the thirsty men and stock.

In all, thirty-five days were required for the thirty men, forty ox-drawn wagons, fifteen cows and the several riding animals to complete the journey. President Bringhurst and others then visited many watering places in Las Vegas Valley before selecting a settlement site. The location chosen was four miles east of the Las Vegas Springs on an eminence overlooking the lower end of the valley.

On the morning of the second day in camp, a Sunday, the men built a small willow bowery to shade themselves from the heat. In the afternoon it became a meeting room for singing and praying, as well as speechmaking. Captain Rufus Allen said that he would explore the Colorado River at its nearest point to Las Vegas, 28 miles southeast, to determine its navigability for steamers. That group returned less than a week later with an unfavorable report.

Early on the third day in Las Vegas, John Steele began surveying the brush-covered land into fifteen five-acre lots for farms, thus allowing two and a half acres for each man in camp. Smaller quarter acre garden lots were also laid out. On the slope of a fifty-foot bench a few rods south of the creek, a party of men began laying off a 150 foot square fort to be built after crops had been planted. It would have a splendid view in all directions except west. Travelers approaching from California on the emi-

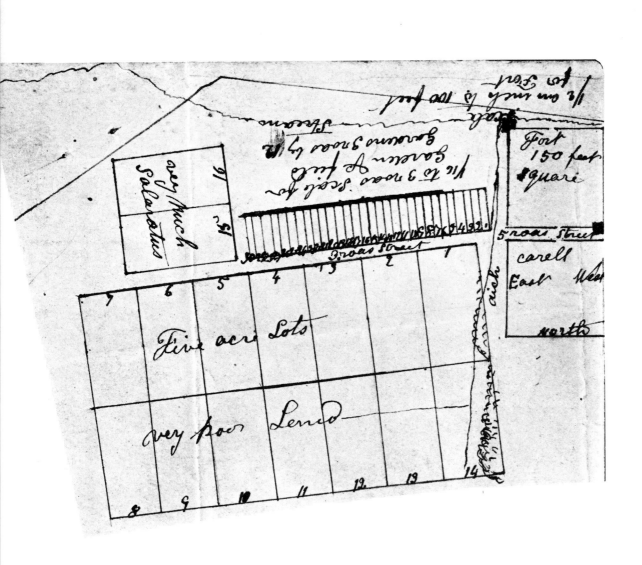

On June 19, 1855 John Steele of Las Vegas wrote in his diary, "I went to work and plumbed the north star and got the range and laid out the fort 150 foot square." It is shown on both of Steele's maps, reproduced below. To the left of the fort (opposite page) are slender rectangular numbered garden plots, one for each settler. Below them are five-acre farm lots each worked by two men. The map below depicts Las Vegas as a small island of settlement in a vast sea of worthless desert. North (left) of the fort were "correll" and "adobies". To the east of the fort were farm and garden plots. South (right) of the fort is Las Vegas Creek which flowed through a "tooly grass" area, two and one-half miles long and one-half mile wide. Also prominent on the map is a vast mesquite forest extending from the fort down Las Vegas Wash to the base of Sunrise (Frenchman) Mountain and spreading out toward the Colorado River, beyond the upper right corner of the map.

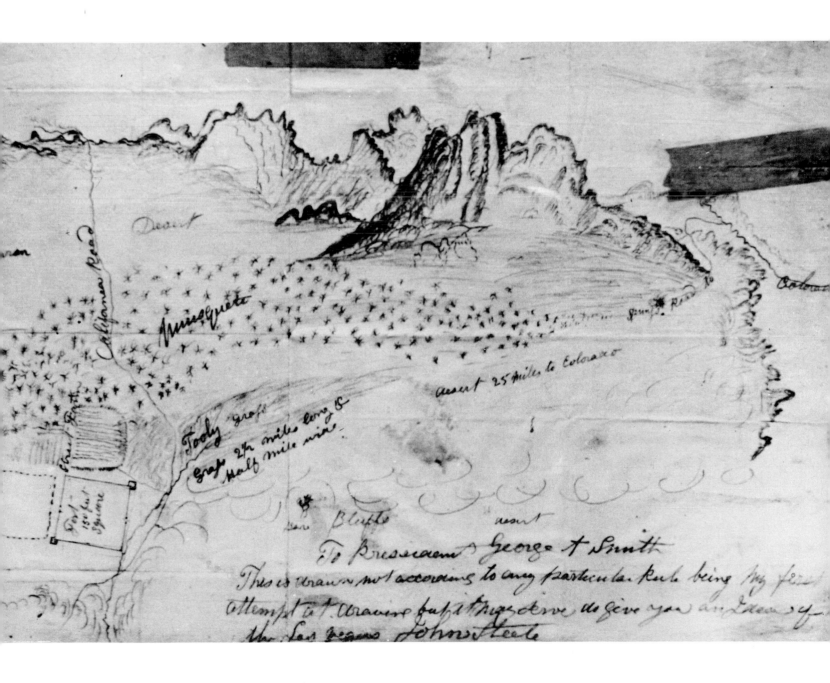

grant road would not be able to see the settlement until they were about a hundred yards from it.

A couple of men began digging ditches to facilitate irrigation. Others spent nearly a week clearing land below the camp of mesquite and other brush and began planting gardens. The Las Vegas missionaries had come expecting to harvest a crop that summer to sustain themselves through their first winter.

This division of work was carried to a logical extreme. For instance, when two of the missionaries accompanied Captain Allen to the Colorado River, others did their work in their absence. When a man had to leave his work to take his turn as herdsman to drive the stock or perform guard duty, his work was shared among the others. The mission's very survival depended on this close social contact.

Shortly after the Mormons arrived in Las Vegas Valley, the leaders met with area Indian chiefs to seek their approval to settle the land. Since in preceding years, some emigrants had murdered Indians without provocation, their antagonism and hatred for the white man had been aroused. The Mormons hoped to reach an agreement to respect each other's rights and insure peace. Bringhurst realized that if his men mistreated the Indians, they would seek revenge at the first opportunity.

Throughout the area the Paiutes lived in wickiups which were generally used only one season and rebuilt again. In the winter they lived in the valleys near springs, subsisting principally on seeds, roots, rodents, lizards and roasted agave. During the late summer and fall most of the Paiutes were in the mountains harvesting pine nuts. The small Indian clans laid claim to various area resources such as a thicket of mesquite trees or a section of pine trees.

On the next Sunday, June 24, a missionary party returning from the Pacific Islands edified their Las Vegas brethren with testimonials, prayers, and English and Hawaiian hymns. About thirty well-behaved Indians from near the Snow Mountain (Mount Charleston) attentively listened to the preaching, although they did not understand it.

In months to come many other missionary groups passed through Las Vegas. The settlers always asked the wayfarers to relate their experiences in spreading the Mormon gospel in far away places. Many others, including mail riders, trading parties, and various emigrants, including apostate Mormons enroute to California, all paused here to rest and replenish water supplies before moving on.

At daybreak on the morning of July Fourth the Las Vegas missionaries were awakened by three firearm salutes from Captain John Steele's Las Vegas Guards, organized only the day previously to furnish protection from the Indians. With no cannon available the guards created additional noise by "shooting off" the anvils. After powder was poured into a hole or surface of one upright anvil, another was inverted and placed on top. A fuse was then attached, and mud was applied to seal the space between the irons. When the fuse was ignited it blasted the anvils apart, resulting in a boom as loud as a cannon shot or a thunder clap. The echo startled the nearby sleeping Indians, letting them know that something unusual was going to happen.

Early that same afternoon, President Bringhurst offered a prayer, and two hours later a crude flag was raised while the guards saluted it with guns and cheers. Steele made the flag by tearing white cloth and red flannel into strips and added a blue field. The thirty-foot pole consisted of a false wagon tongue, a willow pole and a mesquite stump all spliced together. Mid-afternoon was spent in singing national and religious songs and in giving speeches and toasts. Later the mission clerk noted in his diary, "What was remarkable on such a day, not a drunken, disorderly man was seen."

Anticipating the arrival of the California mail rider who would stop here on his way to Utah, Bringhurst on July 10 wrote the following letter to a friend in Salt Lake City: "Our crops look remarkably well; we think we can see the corn grow, at any rate it does grow one and one-half inches in 24 hours ... The health of the camp is generally good and the weather very warm."

The hot weather prevented a long work day. Instead of using light clothing to labor in the summer sun, the men wore heavy wool garments. Unbearably hot winds swept the valley as though they had emerged from a furnace. The barren uninviting surroundings moved one missionary to write that "the country around here looks as if the Lord had forgotten it." Only in the cool stream and in the springs above the settlement did the men find relief.

Most of each day the men hoed and worked along the rows of corn and vegetables in the sandy soil moistened by small irrigation ditches. John Steele spent his spare time in studying the Indian language and in reading the best publications he could find, such as Mitchell's Geography, Peter Parley's History of Nations, a history of England and other smaller books.

With the crops growing well in mid-July, the men turned their attention to public works about the settlement. Certain men were appointed to perform particular tasks, and the clerk kept accurate accounts of work time. Everyone was expected to labor equally.

Later in July Bringhurst called out the names of eight men to accompany him to the mountains on a weekend trip to explore for timber for building improvements. Enough pine was hauled back to build three bridges across the creek that flowed alongside. With every available man pitching in the work was finished in a day.

At the same time others began fencing the farms. After digging foot deep trenches the men tossed into them native thorny mesquite brush and shoveled the dirt back into place, leaving the tops of branches exposed. This barricade not only discouraged Indian foot traffic into the fields, but also warded off jackrabbits and wandering stock. When working with mesquite the men wore a heavy shirt and buckskin pants and mittens.

The next project, completed in three days' time, was an adobe brick corral "eight rods wide by 150 feet" alongside the fort site. Thereafter, each man's stock was kept in a certain area inside the corral after the animals had grazed in the nearby grassy meadow during the day.

When Bringhurst announced another timber-searching expedition a few days later, discord developed in the mission. He had called for five men to prepare for the trip and asked that others loan animals, but only one man volunteered to go and one other offered mules. Bringhurst then gave his brethren a severe lecture on selfishness in not making available their animals for those going out for the benefit of the mission. The men relented and horses were provided and hastily assembled. A five-man party found stands of excellent timber thirty-five miles west, but the vast stretches of sand and gravel between the settlement and the mountains meant that a wagon road had to be built.

Throughout August the men prepared hundreds of sun-baked adobe bricks to build the fort walls. Construction began on September 4, and within a week they had made great progress on the walls, which had a base two feet thick, rising from a sturdy stone foundation. At the same time construction started on dwellings inside the fort, and by the middle of September the sides of the President's house were finished.

For the next few months work continued at intervals on the fort, and by November many of the unfinished houses were occupied. Late in February of the next year, 1856, the 14-foot wall in front of the fort was completed, as well as those nine feet high on the other three sides. The top of each wall was a foot in width. Inside the fort eight two-story houses and storage buildings facing inward formed part of the walls. Good substantial gates had also been built and the bastions on the northeast and southwest corners of the fort were finished. Later a slope of clay packed around the base of the fort drained rain water away.

Agricultural development that first year met with varying success. The corn which had been planted soon after their arrival was ready late in August, though the blackbirds claimed part of it. Early in September melons were ripe on the vine, and these foods broke the monotony of the scanty summer diet of mostly bread and water and an occasional cup of coffee. Though the field crops grew well at first and "bid fair to come to maturity by frost", the weeds and heavy alkali content in the soil killed much of the peas and bean crops. The oats survived that first season fairly well. Other types of garden crops and even "tobacco and cotton were grown quite extensively," according to a contemporary government report of the area.

Work conditions improved late that first year after the men began using horses obtained in California. Five of the missionaries had traveled there in September to trade thirty head of Utah cattle and some of their wagons for horses and mules. They received $100 for a good wagon but only $53 for a yoke of cattle. Since the first crop generally failed, late in November the men had to begin plowing anew for planting vegetables and spring grains. Additional lands were cleared at the same time.

Relations with the area Paiutes never developed into hostilities; the missionaries dealt their neighbors a firm but respectful hand. They were generally well behaved, yet frequent theft made the Mormons ever watchful of their possessions. Anyone guarding the cattle during the daytime carried a gun fired only in case of alarm; at night the animals were herded into the corral. All provisions were kept in wagons until buildings in the fort were completed.

Nevertheless, the red man was often hungry, and the Mormons' grain fields proved to be a great temptation. They went into them at night and helped themselves to what they liked best. After the thefts got out of hand, the men posted a guard

Late in the summer of 1855 the Mormon missionaries built a 150 foot square fort at a site near the modern intersection of Las Vegas Boulevard North and Washington Avenue. It was on a hill overlooking several small farm plots. In this painting Indians are making adobe brick out of mud and grass. After the bricks were baked in the sun, the missionaries extended the walls which are two feet thick at the bottom and tapering at the top and fourteen feet high on the south side, shown here. On the corner is one of the fort's two bastions. Leading off the picture's left edge is the east fort wall; the gate braced by the timber is incorrectly placed in that location in this painting.

At left one man uses a team of oxen and sleigh to haul building stone to the fort. In front of him another man is trimming logs hauled from the Spring Mountains. With no women at the mission in 1855 the men had to prepare their own coffee; a steaming pot is just beyond the logger. As a result of their long and arduous work, the men's arms bore deep red scratches inflicted while clearing the land of thorny mesquite trees and erecting mesquite fences around the fields. As aids, the missionaries only had forty wagons and ox teams, fifteen cows and Indian laborers.

24

to protect their fields. Flour was taken from the wagons and meat also was stolen.

John Steele, in writing to Salt Lake City about Indian behavior, stated "Really I do not blame them for stealing anything to eat, for there is not anything in all this country for them to eat except mesquite and lizards. The wolves here are as thin as a grey hound that has had nothing to eat for two months...These are the facts." Yet Steele remarked about the friendliness of the natives and how they would work hard for the colonists at any laborious job in exchange for old clothing and food, especially squash. The Indians also assisted in building the fort walls.

At the same time the Mormons were constantly doing missionary work, and many Indians agreed to be baptized into the Mormon church, at least in part so that they could secure gifts of clothing and food. On November 4 about seventy Indians attended a Sunday meeting where fifty-six men, women and children were baptized. Brigham Young had decreed that the "Lamanites" (Indians) had to wash themselves before the Mormon leaders could administer baptism. Climaxing the ceremony, each convert was given an Anglicized name, usually biblical.

Mormons frequently called the natives "Lamanites" because the Book of Mormon refers to the surviving race of ancient Americans by that curious name. They are described as part of the ancient house of Israel which had migrated to the Americas in about 600 B.C. Most modern anthropologists, however, agree that the existing evidence does not justify a lineage connecting the American Indian with the Jew.

On each Sunday throughout the year the missionaries held religious services. The best singers were organized into a choir, and the other men took turns at preaching on any topic they chose, even if it were not of a religious nature. A prayer meeting was held on Thursday. Lectures on various subjects also were heard at weekly meetings of the Las Vegas Lyceum, founded in December of that first year as a cultural organization.

As spiritual leader of the mission, President Bringhurst occasionally engaged in hard preaching to improve the morale and the performance of duties by the missionaries. On one occasion he noted that some men had become so engrossed with their own speaking that the listeners got in the habit of nodding. Bringhurst reminded his brethren that "it was as easy to preach the spirit of God out of a man as it was to preach it into him." He wanted the breth-

When Las Vegas Mission thrived during 1855-58, Brigham Young presided over the Mormon Church and governed the Utah Territory. This dynamic leader played a most significant role in westward expansion and settlement, establishing a theocracy in the desert. A polygamist with twenty-seven wives, Young was called by a contemporary "the most married man I had ever met."

ren to govern their own spirits and avoid lulling others to sleep.

On another occasion Bringhurst noted the waywardness of many of the men and thundered to the backsliders: "The spirit of grumbling, fault finding, laziness, and cussing around that has been going on for some time past [must] be put to an end. ...Those who are determined to lay around and do nothing are as clogs to the wheel and will forthwith get a passport for home, unless they speedily repent and take the proper course..." Dismissal would have been disgraceful indeed.

Legitimate opportunities to leave the mission arose from time to time when permission was obtained. That first fall in Las Vegas, John Steele wrote a letter to a Salt Lake City friend. In it he described the sacrifices he had to undergo in staying in Las Vegas: "I should like very much to go home this fall as my family are completely destitute of the comforts or even the necessities of life, on account of my crops, that I worked very hard to put in before I came away, being completely destroyed by the grasshoppers... When I hear there is no meal in the barrel, and the bishop has none, and no money to buy any with in the treasury, it makes me feel as if my little babies are hungry."

After securing permission, a party of eleven missionaries traveled to Utah on November 8, 1855. They agreed to return to Las Vegas in about four months, but after returning to that fairer land all of them eventually secured Brigham Young's permission to remain in Utah. Mission personnel was thus reduced to only seventeen, just five months after their arrival.

On Christmas Day about twelve of the men mounted their horses and hunted coyotes in the desert while others played ball in the fort. These were the first recorded instances of their engaging in sports. One man joined Bringhurst in locating the "Indian farm" beside a creek two miles from the fort. This was done as part of a previous agreement with the Paiutes. That same night some Indians entered the unfinished portion of the fort, tore away loose adobe bricks out of sections of two houses and carried away several squash and some corn, all without arousing the guard's notice.

When the year 1856 began, Las Vegas Mission appeared to be making great strides toward permanency. Four additional men arrived

Above are the pages of John Steele's Diary of 1856, now preserved in the Mormon Church Historian's Office. Note that the missionaries traveled directly to the lead deposit as if its existence were already known; no claim is made to an original discovery. Other contemporary Mormon diarists such as William Bringhurst, George Bean and Lorenzo Brown, all mention the lode in the same way as Steele. Who

the Lead region where upon I started again and took along with me some of the boys and piloted Brother Jones to the mines to the mines again he said it was good ore but not in sufficient Quantities to justify working after returning to Camp another Indian by the name of Colorado Came to me I told me he knew where there was more Lead on the California road about one days ride from here accordingly I got up a company for Brother Jones found him Horses & men & Started about the Eleventh of May and found a very flatering prospect there the Company then returned and Jones called on an out fit of Mules & Men & provisions to go and explore the Silver Mountain accordingly of Ebut Knapp W. C. Mitchel or afterwards John Turner & Reson Lewis Started also the Company found them 30 pounds of flower and board them all the time they ware here I Started them on their journey But they returned unsuckcessful on account of the hot

initially discovered ore at the Potosi mine is not now known. Since the Potosi is only four and one-half miles from the Spanish Trail (called the "California Road" by Steele), it is likely that an inquisitive muleteer of a Mexican trading caravan before 1848 probably found the lode and named it after the famous rich Bolivian mine of that day or a much older Potosi mine in the Spanish Pyrenees.

to strengthen the mission, and the new crops and shade trees were growing. The nearly finished fort, when under a strict guard, offered the men security for their possessions from the Indians who became quite adept at stealing. Still, peace and good will prevailed between the white and red man.

On January 10 the mission received documents which allowed the establishment of an official post office, named for its leader Bringhurst. It was not called Las Vegas because a town with that name already existed near Santa Fe in the eastern end of New Mexico Territory.

At about that same time the missionaries bargained with a traveler returning to San Bernardino to obtain for them grape cuttings, fruit trees and seeds from California. On February 25 he returned with wagons loaded with about 1300 grape cuttings alone, and the men began planting the next day. A thousand stems and twigs had been ordered at the rate of $10 per 100.

During the church's February 1856 conference at Salt Lake City, twenty-seven new members were called to strengthen Las Vegas Mission. Probably only about a third of them actually moved to Las Vegas. Late in February, President Bringhurst and three others left the mission to visit their Utah homes, making the trip safely in about four weeks.

That spring the men, in addition to plowing and planting their own crops, also developed the "Indian farm" laid out earlier. They hoped that this gesture to the Indians would reduce depredations. Early in April five missionaries who returned to Utah were replaced by four others arriving at the mission. John Steele took temporary charge of the mission in Bringhurst's absence.

Nathaniel V. Jones was a Mormon church officer in India and Singapore before Brigham Young sent him from Salt Lake City to superintend operations at Potosi.

On April 19 some Indians invited the men to visit their country where lead ore croppings could be found. Two days later a Paiute guide led John Steele and other men to several places in the mountains including eventually to the base of a 150-foot perpendicular cliff near the summit of Potosi Mountain, twenty-seven miles southwest of Las Vegas. There they found ore in "huge quantities" and returned to Las Vegas two days later packing 180 pounds of lead ore.

Early in May Nathaniel V. Jones was sent from Salt Lake City to Las Vegas to investigate the possibility of exploiting the ore for use in "Deseret." He carried a letter from President Young which authorized him to call on the supplies as well as animals and men at Las Vegas Mission to help him in exploring for minerals. Though wood was found near the Potosi mine, the closest running stream was twelve miles away. Less than a mile north of the mine they found a mound spring for camp purposes. During initial prospecting some ore was uncovered, but with summer approaching Jones returned home rather than carry out lead mining operations in hot weather.

Meanwhile, travelers continued to stop at the fort to rest and have their animals shod. Some arrived on foot, accompanied by a horse or mule which packed their possessions. Other better outfitted trains drove herds of animals along the Salt Lake Trail. As usual, the monthly mail rider from Salt Lake City brought copies of the *Deseret News* to subscribers in Las Vegas. That paper was the mission's principal source of outside information.

Late in May three Las Vegas missionaries brought their families to the mission, the first time that women and children began to live at the fort. Two other families arrived in the heat of the summer. Additional ditches were dug and farmland laid out for the new settlers.

When Bringhurst returned on July 7, the men were busy harvesting wheat and oats and planting beans and corn. After surveying the mission's progress, he corrected deficiencies and exhorted the men to fulfill their duties. Later that same month Bringhurst and ten others organized a company to work the lead mines. By the first of August the missionaries had a mild case of the mining fever.

Besides provisions, the men at the fort sent six yoke of cattle and three wagons with tools to make a road to the mines and dig out a spring to obtain water. They uncovered a lead ore body about a foot deep before returning to Las Vegas because a lack of blasting powder prevented further operations. Meanwhile, Nathaniel Jones had left Salt Lake City with three men, two four-mule teams and mining implements. It was inevitable after Jones' arrival on August 8 that a clash of wills between him and Bringhurst would materially affect the mission.

Jones had blasting powder among his supplies. He also possessed a letter from President Young which gave him the authority to ask for assistance of men and supplies from the mission. Bringhurst was not very enthusiastic about using his settlers' scant provisions on these strangers when his own men could have done the mining just as well.

Bringhurst bluntly told Jones that he would not release men and supplies until he had received proper documents ordering him to do so. Lengthy arguments ensued. Several Las Vegans sided with Jones, while others hesitated to leave for the mines without Bringhurst's consent. Since both seemed to have similar authority over the men, the two leaders agreed to write one letter to President Young to have him clarify authority. With Bringhurst's consent Jones then departed for the mines with six men and provisions.

Before that letter reached Salt Lake City, another from Brigham Young addressed to Bringhurst arrived in Las Vegas on August 19. It plainly said that Jones had the authority to superintend the lead mining and call for assistance in carrying out the operation. In anticipation of success, three teams with heavy wagons would soon be sent from Salt Lake City to haul lead ore out of Las Vegas.

That same month a school was started at Las Vegas when two teachers were chosen. Late in August the wife of one of the teachers gave birth to a daughter, Zelpha Deadeura Fuller, the first white child born in southern Nevada. The Indians continued to make night raids on the corn, and worms also were at work on the crops.

In mid-August Jones began mining. Since the lode was located high on a steep mountainside, animals could not transport the ore effectively until an adequate pack trail could be built. One of the local missionaries, Lorenzo Brown, thought that such a job would cost a thousand dollars. Instead, Jones hired Indians as beasts of burden to pack 10,000 pounds of ore in exchange for ten shirts and food. The natives hauled only one load of rock on their backs and left their jobs.

On a hillside a few yards north of Potosi Spring, Jones began constructing a smelter, although probably no one in his party had ever seen an active lead mine or furnaces, according to Lorenzo Brown, who expressed much displeasure over the project.

Except for the adobe bricks, materials for building the smelter had to be hauled more than six miles. Two furnaces or chambers were constructed, each about three and a half feet in length and width and about five feet high. In the back of each chamber was an opening large enough for logs to be dropped. A small hole in front would allow the molten lead to run out.

On September 10 the new smelter was fired up. About 2000 pounds of ore were shoveled into each chamber which was then filled with logs and set on fire. But the men soon found out that the furnace walls could not stand the blast. Jones then left for home to obtain better building materials for building new furnaces.

During October other Las Vegas missionaries attempted to smelt Potosi ore. From 4000 pounds of mineral they recovered only twelve iron pigs of fifty pounds each. In another operation another 4500 pounds of ore yielded only eight pigs. It was hard work hauling logs in the bitter cold through

William Bringhurst, a political and academic leader in Utah before assuming the Presidency of Las Vegas Mission, became embroiled in the Potosi controversy and left in disgrace.

rugged mountains to feed the furnace, and late in October snow began to fall. Brown, with a wry sense of humor, reported that the miners ate pancakes and tea for supper and had tea and pancakes for lunch, "so that they would have a variety." He added that tea made of desert brush made a tasteful beverage.

In the meantime, the Bringhurst-Jones controversy over Potosi mine continued to trouble the men, and Bringhurst called for a vote of confidence to determine who desired to continue under his leadership. Everyone had a chance to speak his feelings. Three men declared that they were against Bringhurst. Days later the mission leader showed that the strain of the uncertainty and his many problems had worn down his patience. Although he had advised gentle treatment of the natives, Bringhurst kicked an Indian from his house and out of the fort for stealing bread and other items.

Early in November dissension developed anew because of a proposal to build a $1000 house of worship, eighteen by twenty-six feet in size. The men were divided again, particularly in raising funds for it. One faction thought that they should repair the fences first and was content to worship in Bringhurst's house which had been used as the meeting place for more than a year. Despite some protests a tax of $38 per person eventually was decided upon, and work started on the building when two men began hauling stones for the foundation.

Two men on their way to California brought bad news on November 12. They informed Bringhurst that Brigham Young had released all the missionaries then visiting in Utah. Those remaining in Las Vegas carried on the work of maintaining the fort, but there was much discontent. Indians continued raids on the grain and cattle, and leadership problems persisted. When grievances again were aired at a meeting two weeks later, Bringhurst said that he had no desire for any man to pity him because he did not at all feel sorry for himself.

In December Nathaniel Jones returned from Utah with three wagons filled with supplies and apparatus for smelting, including bellows, a furnace, hearths and an assortment of tools, to begin development of the lead "diggings". Jones also delivered a letter from President Young to Samuel Thompson authorizing him to become president of Las Vegas Mission in place of Bringhurst. In a letter to Bringhurst, Young stated the reasons he had been relieved of his job and disfellowshipped from the church.

Since both men had friends and followers, the leadership change caused much dissatisfaction, and nearly everybody was on the verge of leaving. Thompson asked for a vote of the men to see if they were willing to sustain him as president. Only three men declined to follow the new leadership in addition to Bringhurst, who left for California a week later.

During December Jones and eight other men at the mines spent about two weeks in erecting a crude adobe furnace at Potosi Spring. A wooden frame was built to set the horse-powered bellows in place, and fire bricks were prepared. Other men cut wood with which to make charcoal, an agent in smelting lead ore. After a trail had been constructed, a mule train began packing lead ore down a 700 foot descent from the mine, three-eighths of a mile south of the furnace. Four Paiutes also packed mineral in exchange for pants. They walked barefoot through the snow instead of wearing their valuable moccasins.

Jones fired up the new furnaces on Christmas Day but the metal proved hard to smelt. Nevertheless the men labored hard, and a few wagonloads of lead soon left the mines for Cedar City, Utah. All smelting was done at the mines; none of the ore was hauled by ox-team to Las Vegas for treatment in a smelter, as some have written.

After five weeks of naive operations Jones decided to give up on the Potosi mine late in January 1857. In all about 9000 pounds of lead had been produced, but it was too flaky and brittle on account of its high zinc and silver content, which Jones and other Mormons did not recognize. California miners at Potosi in 1861 determined the ore's composition. Nevertheless, Jones' attempt at lode mining and smelting was a first within modern Nevada, two and a half years before the famed Comstock Lode was discovered at Virginia City in the northern part of the State.

The mineral yield of about twenty to thirty percent proved to be of a much poorer quality than the men had expected. Underneath the rich surface minerals they found in the rock much "dry bone, black jack and sulphur" which hindered the smelting process. Threat of property destruction by the Indians, a shortage of animals, and a lack of water and grass to sustain the animals also led to abandonment of the operation. The mules were fed only three pints of oats per day, and were so nearly starved that they resorted to eating their own dung. When the men sent their animals into the desert sage, they would gnaw at rawhide ropes or anything else used to tie them. The men's fare consisted chiefly of bread and sometimes a stew of squash or boiled beans. A few had butter and pork.

Jones and others left Las Vegas for Salt Lake City with the mail rider on February 18. His operations were one of the few instances in which the Mormon pioneers practiced mining. The dozen or so wagon loads of metal had been traded in the Utah towns for goods badly needed at the mission.

Mormon church officials finally terminated Las Vegas Mission in mid-February 1857. Most of the men rejoiced when Brigham Young's letter came to Las Vegas on February 23 granting the men their liberty. The colonists had endured all they could of hard work, lack of good food and bad weather. In its issue of February 25, the Deseret News listed for the last time a Las Vegas distributing agent for its newspaper.

During the next several days most of the men prepared for moving. Two men were sent to the mines to retrieve a cart to carry property back to

Utah. Though they found it intact, the Indians had already burned the roof of a rock house and destroyed other improvements.

The general exodus began on March 23, 1857, thus practically dissolving Las Vegas Mission. The Indians were very much opposed to the men leaving the valley. Until released more formally, a few missionaries decided to stay and help the Indians as much as possible. Efforts toward evangelizing the Indians were dropped entirely.

Several months later—in February 1858—an eleven-man Mormon party traveled to Las Vegas. "There we left five men to smelt some lead; 300 pounds of ore brought 140 pounds of good lead made in a little adobe furnace," wrote one of the men. While this single recorded instance of 1858 area smelting activity probably took place inside the Las Vegas fort walls, the furnace may well have been situated below the mine where the earlier ones were. The Potosi Mine in contemporary writing was occasionally called the "Vegas Mines".

All during the spring and summer of 1858 the Indians and the few Las Vegas settlers raised more than forty acres of wheat and corn. But when the crops were ready for harvesting in September, the natives swooped down on the fields and carried them off entirely. Later that same month at a special church conference at Santa Clara, Utah, it was decided to abandon Las Vegas as a mission and settlement. Yet, Las Vegas Mission paved the way for later Mormon settlement of southern Nevada after 1864.

Contrary to general opinion the mission did not end because Salt Lake City was about to be overrun by General Albert Johnston's federal military forces. This did not occur until June 26, 1858, more than fifteen months after most of the Las Vegas missionaries had left in March 1857. At that time Salt Lake City basked in peace; the authorities there did not even feel the threat of an invasion until the summer of 1857 and Brigham Young did not declare martial law in Utah until September 15. By that date federal troops had begun their march from Fort Leavenworth, Kansas, toward Utah.

The extensive and varied reasons why Las Vegas Mission failed include: a lack of supplies, dissension over lead mining operations, uncertainty of the mission's leadership, inability to solve social problems, laborious and unsuccessful missionary efforts among the Indians, and an insufficiency of good cropland or an unwillingness to expand it. The public works program did not succeed because duties were not shared equally. In the mission's first six months several men had logged in twelve to fifteen days of community work while others had participated as little as one day.

Religious instruction to the Indians failed miserably, especially from the moral standpoint. Despite gifts that the Mormons dispensed freely, the natives relied on their natural inclination to steal instead of working as the church had taught. An itinerant Mormon missionary who passed through Las Vegas in December 1858 humorously remarked, "There seems to be but very little 'Mormon' in them, and they showed me on their finger nails how much."

CHAPTER THREE

Potosi and Fort Baker

AFTER THE MORMONS ABANDONED LAS VEGAS IN SEPtember 1858, the well-built stockade and cabins were left to the elements. Emigrants and nomadic Indians destroyed many of the improvements and used the mesquite fences for firewood. Vegetable gardens and grain fields became a jackrabbit feeding ground, and even the shy coyote freely moved about the crumbling adobe walls, while great horned owls hooted from the gatepost. Still, increased numbers of freighting outfits and mail carriers traveling between Los Angeles and Salt Lake City continued to make rest stops at this tree-shaded spot.

Early in 1859 the Los Angeles *Star* reported that a huge train of sixty wagons loaded with dry goods, groceries, hardware, boots and shoes, valued at between $60,000 and $70,000, had left the coast for Salt Lake City. That year at least three major firms brought goods to the Mormon capital.

Newspapers in Los Angeles expressed an interest in improving the road to Utah, thereby capturing more of its trade. Whereas snow sealed off the freight road from San Francisco over the Sierra to Utah during the winter, the Los Angeles-Utah road through Las Vegas remained open throughout the year. It led through grass-covered valleys, and ample supplies of wood and water could be found throughout, except for the fifty-five mile dry stretch between Las Vegas and the Muddy River to the northeast.

The early 1860's proved to be significant for the Las Vegas area. At that time San Franciscans and others in West Coast cities were caught up in a mining fever brought about by the development of the fabulous Comstock Lode at Virginia City. Thus any discovery east of the Sierra was heralded as a rich mining country. When in August 1860 a California prospecting party brought attention to the abandoned Potosi Lode, twenty-seven miles southwest of Las Vegas, the newly-formed Colorado Mining Company reopened the mine early in December.

Late that same month a Los Angeleno noted a number of experienced Mother Lode miners in town outfitting for trips to the Potosi lead mine, or "Las Vegas Silver Mines" as it also was called. One party had left ore reduction machinery on the San Pedro docks for later transport to the new boom. Clay was found near the mines for making fire brick for the erection of furnaces, and early in 1861 a smelter was blown in at Potosi Spring.

Miners who had rushed from San Francisco paid approximately $70 fare on an ocean steamer to Los Angeles and for the jolting six-horse stage across mountains and deserts to Potosi. Most coaches also carried letters and newspapers. Freighters charged from eight to eleven cents a pound to haul merchandise from the coast to the mines.

Some of the Potosi miners, when returning to Los Angeles for provisions, showed off silver ore specimens, and this added to the delirious excitement over the desert mines. Additional mining companies quickly organized to issue stock and raise money for development, while prospectors searched for overlooked leads. The *Southern News* in Los Angeles noted the necessity of improving the wagon road through Cajon Pass to accommodate the increasing number of mine boomers.

Amid the "numerous, large and well-defined lodes" at Potosi, promoters laid out a townsite between two mountain spurs about five miles south of the Salt Lake Trail. The entire district was in the northwest tip of New Mexico Territory. A former Mother Lode printer, J.A. Talbott, made longhand copies of a newspaper with the colorful title of *East of the Nevada; or the Miner's Voice from the Colorado*. From his ranch in Las Vegas, Captain Jere Stevens, president of the Colorado Mining Company, issued his own manuscript sheet, the *Potosi Nix Cum Rouscht*, but it was also short-lived.

At the beginning of spring 1861 one man noted as many as thirty-five miners arriving at Potosi daily, in addition to about eight large teams of six to ten mules drawing wagons heavily loaded with groceries, provisions and mining tools such as powder, drills, hammers, and crowbars. Assays on selected ore ran from $400 to $900 per ton in silver in addition to 800 to 1500 pounds of lead. Many looked to the muddy Colorado River as a possible avenue of transportation for shipping supplies in and hauling out ore and concentrates to the West Coast.

Demand for fresh produce was partially satisfied by some of the miners who settled nearby and started small gardens. One man who left Potosi with a bottle of whiskey in one hand and a loaf of bread in the other, traveled thirty miles to locate a ranch in Las Vegas Valley. He and others grew vegetables in gardens and peaches in small orchards.

Besides Captain Stevens, others at Las Vegas in 1861 were his brother, William France, and Messrs. Allen, Champlin, Sewell and Cooper. A few men started small farms closer to Potosi. Many of them also sold produce to travelers on the continually active Salt Lake Trail, but none succeeded in establishing a permanent farm in Las Vegas Valley.

All during the spring of 1861 Potosi thrived as a promising district which would in time "surely rival the Comstock Lode" according to one optimistic report. Men of enterprise were there, and Potosi was not a "community of silk-stocking gentry," in the words of an early resident. Occasional entertainment was provided by the local thespians who boasted that they could play "all the way from Macbeth to Toodles."

Prospectors unable to get in on the ground floor at Potosi scattered elsewhere to uncover new bonanzas. In the spring of 1861 Joseph Good (who later settled Goodsprings, Nevada) headed one prospecting party, and mountain man Johnny Moss

another into the steep-walled gorge of El Dorado Canyon on the west side of the Colorado River. Some hungry Paiutes told a party of miners where they might fill their sacks with *oro*, but they were led to worthless rock. Yet on their return trip some of them stuck their picks into the hard-rock veins of El Dorado Canyon and found gold.

Though that district got off to a quiet start, by 1863 nearly every steamer into Los Angeles brought new mining parties destined for the Colorado River districts, including El Dorado Canyon. The common route was by way of Fort Mohave, Arizona, but others arrived there after passing through Las Vegas.

Fort Baker

When the Civil War broke out in 1861, few guessed that Las Vegas would have even a nominal role in it. Since some Confederate strength existed in California, Arizona, and New Mexico, the Union Army military leaders had to devise ways to prevent a possible rebel takeover of any part of the Southwest. Late in 1861 rumors circulated that a large Confederate force existed in southeastern Arizona and was steadily growing in number because of sympathizers from California. The Confederate Flag briefly flew over Tucson late in 1861.

To discourage travel and communication between rebels in California and the South, military authorities announced new restrictions in December 1861. The San Francisco *Mirror* stated that "A line of military posts, extending from Fort Yuma to the upper crossing of the Mojave, is to be established and Fort Mojave [Mohave] reoccupied ...After the posts are established, every thoroughfare leading to the southern states will be closed, and no one allowed to pass without passports from the Commander of the [Army] department."

Others with an interest in the Salt Lake Trail also desired military occupation of the interior desert area, especially at the important Las Vegas stop on the Salt Lake Trail. The Los Angeles *Star* editor argued that "At the Vegas, the troops will be comfortably located near good water, wood and grass; the post will be maintained at a much less cost to the government; the troops will be on hand to protect emigrants from the faithless, thieving, murdering Pah-Utes; they would protect the traders and teamsters conveying merchandise to Salt Lake City from here; and give protection to those enterprising men who are now laboring there to open up and develop that rich mining country."

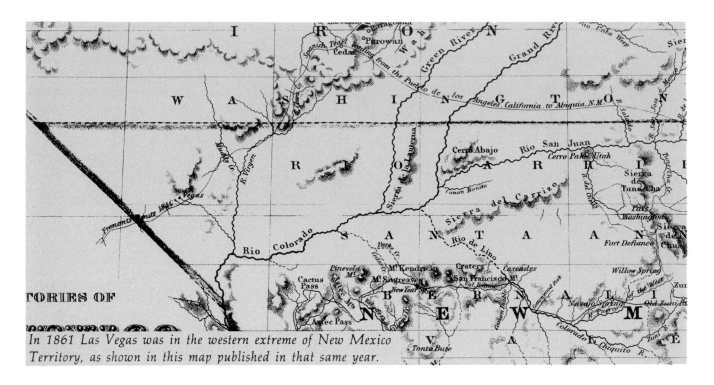

In 1861 Las Vegas was in the western extreme of New Mexico Territory, as shown in this map published in that same year.

For the preceding several months in 1861 the *Star* editor had been carrying an all-out fight with the San Francisco press over the best trade route from the Coast to Salt Lake City. On December 1861 the *Star* declared the Daily Overland Mail a fraud and argued for diversion of the Utah-California mail by way of the Southern Route through Las Vegas at least during the winter months.

Southern contacts received news of California military operations by various correspondents. Newspaper columns also regularly contained accounts of military movements and various rumors which perked the ears of Confederate spies. After February 1862, when the Los Angeles *Star* began to sympathize openly with the South, local pro-Union officials forbade that paper use of the regular mails and the Wells-Fargo & Company Express.

With this climate prevailing, Colonel James H. Carleton, Commander of the First California Volunteers, had to devise a way to conceal his important mission of marching across southern Arizona to New Mexico to regain Confederate held forts and territory. Capitalizing on the rebel *Star's* preoccupation with establishing the Salt Lake Trail through Las Vegas as the main trade route between California and Utah, Carleton late in 1861 issued from his headquarters near Los Angeles an important military circular.

In it he ordered that nine companies of the California Column be transferred to Fort Yuma, California to guard secessionists kept there in confine-

ment. Another seven company expedition would move up the Colorado River, with three of them reoccupying Fort Mohave and reviving the ferry service there. "The other four . . . will proceed on to Las Vegas on the Salt Lake Road to establish a post at the old Mormon fort. . . . The new post will be known as Fort Baker." It would be named for English-born Colonel Edward D. Baker, an Oregon resident who fell while fighting the rebels in Virginia only a few months previous.

Carleton's plan conveniently leaked out of headquarters and was picked up by the California press. The Los Angeles *Southern News* reported early in 1862 that "Fort Mojave [Mohave] would be reoccupied, and a new post established at the Vegas. . . . Both daily overland routes would then be protected." An ocean steamer took the news to San Francisco, where the *Alta* on January 31 described the storms that had wrecked the wagon roads to the Colorado, thus preventing Carleton from moving men and supplies to Forts Mohave and Baker, by way of Fort Yuma. Indeed, vast floods had hit many parts of San Bernardino and Los Angeles Counties. One company of the Colorado River expedition began repairing the road to Fort Yuma.

On March 5 the *Alta*, though confessing the uncertainty of military movements, reported that Carleton "was anxious to have the roads out of Los Angeles to the Colorado River and to Utah in serviceable condition without delay."

Another Los Angeles correspondent to the *Alta*

a week later wrote that "Colonel Carleton is incessantly occupied in getting the expedition on the march...[we know] nothing more of the objects of the expedition than that announced, viz, the occupation of the Colorado River forts and the holding of the Indians in check, so that the great mail may be carried through with dispatch and certainly." He also mentioned that troops were on they way to build Fort Baker and that Carleton's expedition was destined to be in Utah in less than twenty days.

Meanwhile, under the cloak of secrecy and the great storms that ravaged all of California in the winter of 1862, Carleton skillfully organized his confirmed yet undisclosed mission of marching to the Rio Grande in New Mexico and driving out the Confederates. Advance detachments of what became known as the Column from California had left the Los Angeles area as early as February, and that spring Carleton briefly reunited his command at a point on the Gila River in Arizona and at other places as the troops marched across southern Arizona. By keeping his plans to himself all of that spring, Carleton succeeded in camouflaging his objective, though some favorable dispatches made the press.

For instance, one report out of Los Angeles late in March told of government transportation trains continually leaving for the interior. "A large amount of army stores for Fort Baker have been loaded and are now on their way to their destination." Though the materials for the new posts were marked "Fort Mohave" or "Fort Baker", those in charge of stores knew this meant shipping everything to Fort Yuma and points beyond in interior Arizona for the California Column.

Not until the end of April were Carleton's actual movements publicly revealed. One writer stated that "Carleton most wisely kept to his own counsels, bewildering everybody so much that no one dared to guess his movements...The expedition under Colonel Carleton was intended to act against the rebels on the western and southern borders of Texas."

The mere fact that Carleton was marching toward New Mexico made the Confederate forces on the Rio Grande retreat from their strongholds into Texas. In May Carleton (by then elevated to rank of General) established federal authority in all of New Mexico, becoming Commanding General of the Military Department of New Mexico.

A separate northern California volunteer regiment marched to Salt Lake City in mid-May to regarrison forts in Utah and protect the Overland Mail routes in accordance with a Secretary of War order. The item said nothing about Fort Baker. In 1864 Captain George Price's explorers, dispatched from Camp Douglas near Salt Lake City to find a wagon road to the Colorado River, stopped at Las Vegas. In his diary he commented on the fine water and grass. No soldiers were encountered. In fact, all unofficial accounts of travelers through Las Vegas during the Civil War fail to mention a fort or garrison, though the natural advantages of the spot always called for comment.

Thus by remaining inactive, Fort Baker fulfilled a mission for Carleton by diverting attention from his march through southern Arizona during a critical time early in the Civil War. The abandoned Mormon fort buildings garrisoned no troops; there were no bugle calls, no fighting, no improvements made. It is incorrect to refer to the remaining building of the Mormon fort as "Fort Baker."

After the Potosi silver boom subsided late in 1861, many who tried to farm at Las Vegas left their fields for fairer ground. Other individuals lived briefly at Las Vegas in the early 1860's but none succeeded in renewing the farm until 1865, when an El Dorado Canyon miner named Octavius D. Gass and two other men reconstructed the buildings and plowed the old fields for cultivation. The resulting Las Vegas Ranch flourished for the rest of the century and proved to be the valley's first sustaining settlement of historical worth.

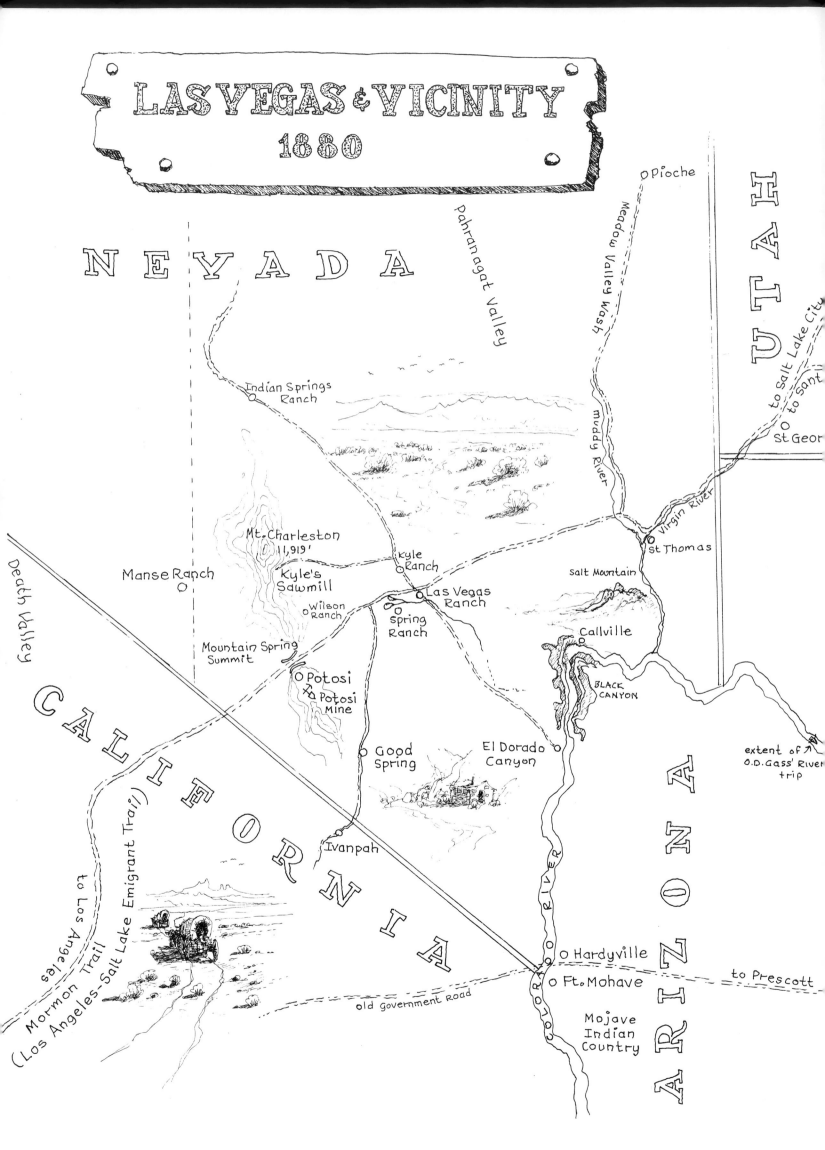

CHAPTER FOUR

Las Vegas Ranch and
Octavius Decatur Gass

SOUTHERN CALIFORNIANS APPROACHING LAS VEGAS from the south on Interstate-15 first see a large sagebrush plain leading to a wide green-gray city that extends the full length of Las Vegas Valley. A century ago wagon travelers and men on horseback following the Los Angeles-Salt Lake Road entered the valley from the southwest after crossing Mountain Spring Summit. They looked upon a long green patch in the middle of the valley. To reach it they followed a crooked trail that wound through dry washes before arriving at Las Vegas Springs at the west end of the oasis.

After pausing beside the tree-shaded springs, travelers of the 1870's moved east along a swift flowing five-foot-wide and two-foot-deep stream arising from the springs. After another three miles they passed the wickiups of nearly 200 friendly Paiutes, and less than a mile further along the creek the big red homemade wagons stopped in front of the adobe ranch house of the extensive Las Vegas Ranch. Opposite the road to the south the stream continued to flow eastward down Las Vegas Wash.

The proprietor of this desert ranch and farm was Ohio-born Octavius Decatur Gass, who left the East coast in 1849 in response to the cry of gold in California. After a long trip around South America's Cape Horn he arrived in San Francisco where he unloaded portable houses and other cargo for $10 a day. Soon thereafter he began mining in the Mother Lode's placer fields of El Dorado County, especially in Merced Canyon. About a year later Gass moved southward to the pueblo of Los Angeles, where in 1854 he enrolled as a member of that town's two year old Masonic Lodge. He was appointed *zanjero* to patrol the open ditches which conveyed water from the Los Angeles River. He saw that no one took too much water and supervised repairs of ditches.

The mineral fever eventually caught Gass again, and by 1859 he had moved to San Jacinto (south of modern Corona, California) to work at the Temescal Tin Mines where he may also have had financial interests. Unsuccessful there, he left after the end of 1860, and beginning in 1862 he enthusiastically mined gold in El Dorado Canyon, the "land of milk and honey and *oro*" on the west bank of the Colorado River, forty miles south of Las Vegas.

Arizona's special June 1864 Territorial census listed this husky six-foot 35-year-old miner as an El Dorado Canyon resident for the preceding eighteen months. During that time he had located sixteen claims, with lodes bearing such names as Buffaloe, Mustang, Apollo and Bucephalus. One local letter writer that same year described Gass as the "worst struck man" with the prospects that he had ever seen. "I don't suppose he would give a man two bits to insure him a fortune in the next two years," the letter said of Gass. But during 1865 he relocated at the abandoned Mormon fort in the middle of Las Vegas Valley.

Gass and other men, especially his early partners Nat Lewis and Louis Cole, rebuilt the wrecked buildings and plowed the fields for new cultivation. A settler named William Knapp operated a store for travelers. These men and others on adjacent homesteads constituted the valley's only permanent residents in the late 1860's but by the mid-1870's some had moved away or Gass had bought them out. When he purchased the nearby 120 acre Spring Ranch in January 1878, Gass thereafter

Octavius Decatur Gass (1827-1924).

owned all of the valley's water and became a virtual king of Las Vegas Valley.

"O.D." often greeted the people passing through. Others in the family and the ranch foreman also met the tired, dusty travelers who first asked where they could camp. They parked their wagons along the creek or at the upper springs, four miles west. At either place there were abundant water and rich bunch grass for their animals. At the springs they found shade and protection under the tall cottonwoods and willows.

Women were especially happy to stop at Las Vegas. They washed and mended clothes beside the springs or along the creek banks while the men repaired the wagons. Often they would bring their horses to be shod at the ranch's blacksmith shop. Larger trains usually had their own blacksmith who fixed horseshoes and welded broken iron parts by using white sand from the bubbling spring. Wagoneers drove into the creek which led from the spring to soak the dry wood of their wheels.

Travelers stayed a day or two, though some required a week or more for rest and repairs before resuming travel across the long waterless deserts. With their buckets and pails swinging from their

hands, the women came to the house asking to buy milk, vegetables and fresh beef which Gass sold at modest prices. Before leaving, many travelers stopped at the ranch house to say good-bye. Some women cried, expressing gratitude for the pleasant interlude in their weary travels, and children gathered around and hugged Mrs. Gass. Most travelers had come to Las Vegas dirty, weary and in need of provisions, and some even with sick children; but they left refreshed, clean and happy.

Inquisitive visitors were shown around the ranch. Entering the main ranch house they saw a large living and dining room extending the width of the house with a twenty-foot table in the middle that sat about fifteen people. It was adorned by a plain oil cloth. For a small sum visitors sometimes ate a meal after the ranch hands and foreman had been served so that they could return to the fields. The family ate last. With so many eating at different hours, it seemed that Lee, the Chinese cook, always had something cooking in the big kettle on the kitchen fire.

Building walls averaged eighteen inches in thickness, tapering at the top, and alongside the windows were portholes about a foot long and six inches high. Off to one end of the house were bedrooms and the kitchen, reached by a separate doorway.

The screenless ranch house back door led directly into the 150 foot square stockade, enclosed by rock fences and buildings. In the 1870's dozens of cattle, horses, about a dozen dairy cows, and a burro were kept there at night. Stables and large haystacks occupied the rear. No trees shaded the bare surface.

The main ranch house occupied the stockade's southwest corner. Directly opposite it and extending north from the southeast corner was a series of about six adobe storage buildings and a blacksmith shop, all of which faced inward. On the south side, connecting the ranch house with the storage buildings, was a high rock wall broken in the center by a gate high enough to allow the largest of wagons and the cattle entry. Its top was braced by a large timber.

South of the stockade and on the other side of the creek were a couple of storage buildings, a wood fence corral and houses of the ranch workers. Heavy wagons rumbled over a sturdy wooden bridge that spanned the creek.

Immediately east grew a willow break. A trail through it led past wild roses and grapevines to fields of alfalfa, grain and corn, as well as shade

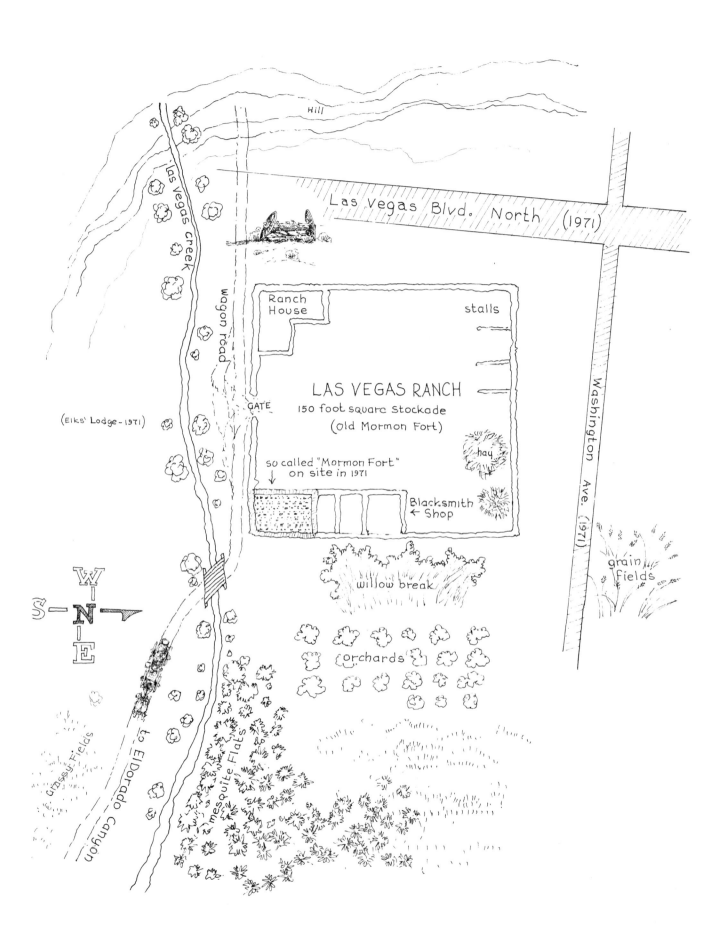

Hill

Las Vegas Blvd. North (1971)

las vegas creek

wagon road

Ranch House

stalls

LAS VEGAS RANCH
150 foot square stockade
(Old Mormon Fort)

GATE

(Elks' Lodge - 1971)

so called "Mormon Fort"
on site in 1971

hay

Blacksmith
← Shop

Washington Ave. (1971)

grain fields

willow break

W
N
S
E

orchards

to ElDorado Canyon

Grassy Fields

mesquite Flats

trees and fruit orchards which included orange, lemon, peach, apple, apricot, fig and pomegranate. In all about 150 acres were in cultivation in 1871, but by the end of that decade irrigated farm land at Las Vegas had been enlarged considerably. Indeed, Gass ran quite a plantation in the midst of a large desert.

Two crops came from the soil annually. It was first sown in small grains—wheat, barley and oats—harvested in late spring principally by Indian women winnowing in the fields with baskets just as in biblical times. The land then was planted in corn, potatoes, beets, cabbage, onions, squashes, melons and other vegetables, especially pink Mexican beans. Gathering and processing about seventy-five acres of beans each fall took several days, requiring the regular hands and about sixty Paiutes, who lived just west of the ranch. They came every morning during the harvest.

Indians pulled and shocked the ripe beans which dried in the fields and then hauled them on a hay-rack into the stockade. On its hard surface they scattered the beans in a circular pile about two feet deep and a hundred feet across. Horses driven around the bean pile trampled it down. As the beans erupted from their shells, the Indians swept them inward and forked the chaff outward. Since the waste was shaken hard before being cast aside, few beans were lost. The dry husks were saved for fodder for the ranch stock.

With most waste removed the beans were run through a small hand-operated fanmill about six feet long, four feet high and three feet wide, which blew away any remaining straw, husk particles and dirt. As the beans were cleaned they rolled into eighty pound sacks. When the harvest ended Gass had hundreds of bean sacks stacked in storage buildings.

Gass paid the Indians with sacks of beans, clothing, sugar and other supplies. The pink beans were a principal part of their diet, along with the native mesquite tree beans which grew in strings about five inches long bunched in heavy clusters. Parts of Las Vegas Valley were a virtual forest of scrubby mesquite trees which grew profusely in the flats between the main ranch house and the Colorado River. Both Mexican and mesquite beans were sweet and nutritious.

Each fall the Paiutes gathered mesquite beans and stored them in their wickiups. After grinding the hard white bean shells between stones with large holes called *metates,* the resulting meal was made into cakes which weighed about ten pounds when dry. Indians packed them for food on their long treks into the nearby Spring Mountains where they picked pinyon nuts. The Indians also killed game, deer, rabbits and mountain sheep. Many Paiutes at Las Vegas and in the Mount Charleston foothills grew corn, pumpkins and melons in small farms and gardens during the summer months.

Most of the Indians wore overalls and a shirt, though some were nearly naked. They regularly bathed above the ranch in a duck pond fed by the creek. Squaws waded into the water with their

PAIUTE BRUSH SHELTERS

dresses on and washed themselves and their children who splashed in the water with them. The Gass family used that same water after it had traveled nearly a mile to the ranch. Because of extensive artesian well drilling in recent years, that stream, later called Las Vegas Creek, dried up soon after World War II.

Paiutes did not bother the travelers who camped in the area. In fact, one squaw occasionally had some fun at their expense. At the bubbling springs, where only heavy objects sank, she would throw her baby into the water, much to the astonishment of travelers. The infant kept afloat by the upward thrust of the artesian water.

Gass' relations with the local Indians were cordial; they helped one another. He and his wife learned Paiute, although many Indians spoke some broken English. Gass had superior weapons, including the only repeating rifle in the area, whereas the Indians only had a few muskets. In the event of depredations the natives understood they would receive swift and severe punishment.

Unfriendly Indians lived in Arizona east of the Colorado River. Late in October 1878 certain "River Indians" (probably Mojaves) entered Las Vegas Valley to fight the local Paiutes because of a long-standing dispute. An Indian runner warned Gass of their coming, and he and his family fled to Ivanpah, a forty mile all-night trip. Riding in a homemade covered wagon, they battled a violent rainstorm and freezing weather to escape. To complicate their plight, the children were already ill with whooping cough before they left the ranch.

Reaching their destination just over the line in California, they were welcomed to the home of a mine operator named C.A. Bidwell and his wife. There Gass met the Yount family from the Manse Ranch in Pahrump Valley, who also had fled from the Indians. At Ivanpah Gass sought additional guns, ammunition and men to protect his property.

When Gass returned he found the undisturbed ranch in the charge of Chief Tecopa, who sat on top of a pile of grain sacks directing the ranch work. The local Paiutes had cared for the stock, milked the cows and churned the butter in Gass' absence. There had been more difficulty with a few local squaw men than with the "River Indians". Since wild grapes grew in the valley, the intruders had

This July 1873 view of Las Vegas Ranch shows the main ranch house before additions were made on its right side. O. D. and Mrs. Gass stand in front of their house. Beyond Mrs. Gass is a storage building that is now called the "Mormon Fort," all that remains of the 1855 construction. In the right foreground beside the cottonwood trees and the creek are Indian children. An unidentified Mormon farmhand is at left.

On March 16, 1876 Frederick S. Dellenbaugh climbed the hill west of the main ranch buildings and sketched this Las Vegas Ranch scene which he later finished in oils. From that same location ranch proprietor O. D. Gass often used field glasses to look over his ranch which extended in the direction of Sunrise (Frenchman) Mountain beyond. A prospector and his pitched tent are in the foreground. On many summer nights the Gass family had no visitors but would awaken surrounded by travelers who had made camp around them during the night. All teams stopped here coming and going east and west. Behind the main ranch house (the building with two windows) is a storage building still on the site in 1971. From it a series of long low storage buildings extend left behind the main ranch house. Still further left are haystacks and horse stalls. During the Mormon ownership (1855-58) the walls contained other houses but Gass removed them to make room for his animals.

Artist and Colorado River historian Dellenbaugh was assistant photographer and artist with Major John W. Powell's Second Expedition through the Southwest in 1871-72. Later he wrote several books including Romance of the Colorado River *and* Fremont and '49.

come to take the harvest from the Paiutes, and to settle old grudges with them. In his day book Gass wrote that the "grape war" was unsuccessful. "It did not pay after they (the River Indians) had a mirror brought before them of their own actions. They curled their tails and slunk off."

Another story which has passed down through the Gass family concerns "O.D." when he was caught nearly defenseless by an insurrection led by one of the local half-breeds. While drinking he had encouraged the local tribe to rise up and demand of Gass more goods for their work on the ranch.

Gass' oldest son, Fenton, later recalled the incident. His father and mother were sitting in the orchard below the main ranch buildings cutting peaches under a large fig tree, when noises came from the direction of the house. His mother guessed that Indians were coming to harm his father.

"O.D." ran along the edge of the break of young willows, back through the rear of the stockade and into the ranch house. Fenton, his sister and his mother took the path to the ranch house. "Mother held our hands while we passed Indians, whom she pushed out of her way as we walked," Fenton said. "Though she did not seem to be afraid, we children cried."

"We have come to see 'Pe-no-kab'" said one Indian chief, ready to announce his ultimatums. That name, meaning "long-back", was given to Gass because of his broad shoulders.

Meanwhile, Gass had dragged his guns and ammunition out of safekeeping and stacked them on the dining table. An old Paiute chief walked toward the house with an armed body guard on either side. With their guns ready, they approached the door. Other armed Indians remained in a flat on the opposite side of the creek.

Gass opened the ranch house door and asked the chief what he wanted.

"We have come to talk."

"If you want to talk, come in here and we'll talk."

When the Indians reached the door, slightly ajar, they peered in and saw the guns and ammunition in plain sight.

Just about that time Gass' Chinese cook violently rang a triangle gong on a high pole ordinarily used to summon the workers to meals.

"Hear that?" Gass exclaimed. "There will be men to get these guns and you won't be able to get anywhere...."

While talking, Mrs. Gass came to the door and threw it open. She grabbed the weapon from one guard's hand and before the other had a chance to recover from the move, she had the gun aimed at his face.

The leader shouted, "Don't shoot! Don't shoot! We want to talk!"

Completely defenseless and defeated, the Indians stacked their weapons alongside the house as Mrs. Gass commanded them to do. Gass and the chief went inside to discuss their problems. Gass told him that there was no reason to quarrel, and in time they came to agreement. As a gesture of peace, they smoked a large meerschaum pipe with a nine-inch stem and a two-inch bowl. The Indian chief puffed on it first and then handed it to Gass, who agreed to give him a horse named Old Doc and a steer. They continued to talk and smoke the peace pipe. Finally the Indians took the animals and left. The local Paiutes were ashamed and later made the half-breed wear a dress and work in the fields with the squaws as punishment. This was the only reported instance of trouble with the local Paiutes that Gass encountered in more than fifteen years at Las Vegas.

Life on The Ranch

Besides the extensive farming, Gass owned about 400 head of cattle tended by Indian cowboys in the grassy fields east of the ranch buildings. No fences contained the cattle to keep them from the grain fields to the north and west. At night the Indians brought the work horses, dairy cows and cattle into the stockade for care and safekeeping. Four or five Mormon ranch hands supervised the Indian herders who also helped prune the orchard and haul in hay. In charge was a foreman who rode horseback over the ranch.

A favorite was Lee, the Chinese cook. While working he wore blue jeans and a blue shirt like most of the other men did, but in his leisure time he preferred Oriental clothing including a skull cap which made his long black hair even more obvious. Lee baked the bread and prepared the meat, using the lesser parts for stews. In the warmer months he had breakfast ready at the first light. Then the men would go to the stables where a couple of Indian stableboys harnessed and hitched animals to equipment for the work planned by Gass and the ranch foreman.

The twice a week butchering of a bull or a cow took place just outside the stockade beneath a large willow tree which had a limb about eight feet from the ground. With no ice available the work had to be done late in the afternoon or early evening.

Las Vegas Ranch's headquarters (above) during both the Gass and Stewart ownership is shown as it appeared around 1905. Much of this building was the southwest corner of the old Mormon fort. Las Vegas Creek flows alongside the row of cottonwood trees at left. Below is the rear of the same house. On the roof is a mission-like bell installed by O. D. Gass in the 1870's after he had it cast in Pioche. Its silvery tones were heard three times daily for nearly a third of a century.

The relationship of the main ranch house with the "old Mormon Fort" in the foreground right is shown above. The Mormons in 1855 initially constructed the latter building (southern Nevada's oldest), but after O. D. Gass remodeled it in the mid-1860's he used it to store beans in large sacks and milk in big pans. Milk was skimmed there and churned in large wooden churns. After 1881 that building was successively owned by Archibald and Helen J. Stewart before the Salt Lake Railroad purchased the grounds in December 1902. In 1930 while preparing plans for construction of Hoover Dam, Bureau of Reclamation engineers repaired the building, poured a concrete floor and occupied it as headquarters for gravel testing for the Dam. In recent years the Daughters of the Utah Pioneers leased the ground and began restorations. In 1970 the City of Las Vegas acquired the building which now contains a small museum display and living quarters for a caretaker. At right the tall cottonwoods almost form a canopy over the "old fort" building.

45

After shooting the animal, the men took a single-tree for a gamblestick and after pinning the hocks, raised the animal off the ground and strung it to the limb. It was splashed down with buckets of water and allowed to cool.

The animal then was skinned, the head removed and carcass butchered into huge sections to be delivered to area mines. After dark a few men hitched a team to a wagon and hurried with the load of beef over the rough fifty mile road to El Dorado Canyon. A detachment of Camp El Dorado soldiers stationed at Las Vegas in 1867-68 also bought beef and produce from Gass. Ivanpah and briefly the Potosi mine also may have been customers. The men made jerky of the leftover beef.

On one occasion while the men were dressing a small steer, an ornery chief from a distant tribe arrived just as the head was being removed. He asked for it, but Gass did not want to give it to him because it was to be delivered to someone else after the brains and tongue had been taken out.

The determined chief picked up a singletree and started to hit Gass over the head with it, but a ranch hand wounded the aggressor with his six-shooter. The fallen Indian crawled along a wide ditch and rested against the side of a fence. After gaining strength he rose on his hands and knees and edged toward the men. The ranch hand fired again and killed the chief. That night one of the ranch hands dragged his body along the road in front of the ranch house, leaving a bloody trail still visible the next morning.

To ease the work of the extensive farm and ranch operations, Gass had plows, a mowing machine, a haypress, tools and the animals. He owned no heavy machinery. At the blacksmith shop plows were sharpened and horses shod. For fire, charcoal instead of stone coal was burned. The sparks would fly when the men applied a big bellows.

Most supplies were brought in by long-line mule or horse team from San Bernardino, though some items were purchased in Pioche, 150 miles north of the ranch. Freighters halted in front of the ranch house to unload various supplies including clothing such as shirts, overalls, red underwear, jumpers, coats, hats, bandana handkerchiefs and shoes, all ordered a month or six weeks earlier. Most of these were sold to travelers, prospectors and workmen; a shirt cost $1.25, overalls were the same price, shoes were $2 a pair and a hat was 75¢.

Many types of dried foodstuffs were brought in including flour, tea, sugar in hundred pound sacks, coffee in fifty pound sacks, canned Boston baked beans, canned blackberries, other canned goods, baking powder, rice, salt, pepper and unparched grain in fifty pound sacks. Mrs. Gass parched the grain by placing it in a pan and cooking it in her wood stove, after which she ground it. Apples, peaches, apricots and other dried fruits grown locally were soaked before cooking.

O.D. Gass — Traveler

During his twenty years in southern Nevada, O.D. Gass made frequent trips to carry out business or look over the area for minerals. In 1864 he, along with James Ferry, a man named Butterfield, and an Indian rowed in either a skiff or a punt from El Dorado Canyon up the Colorado River to a point about twenty miles from the Grand Canyon's mouth. On opposite shores the party erected two low stone monuments.

In 1871, after being briefed by Gass at Las Vegas, members of Lieutenant George Wheeler's survey expedition found one of the markers and removed notes left by the four men. The party in which Gass was a member had not ventured further because they thought additional river travel into the upper Grand Canyon was impossible. In later years before Lake Mead covered the site, a U.S. Geological Survey crew found one of the monuments in 1921.

Early in 1865 Gass regularly led a mule pack train from his El Dorado Canyon home to a salt mountain just south of the Muddy River Valley, about sixty miles northeast. The product was used in milling the ore. In the fall of 1865, by then relocated at Las Vegas, he made a trip as legislator to Arizona's capital, Prescott. There he was reunited with the lawmakers each fall until 1868, when he traveled to Tucson. After 1871 Gass occasionally journeyed to Pioche to pay taxes and visit friends.

On one occasion Gass needed lumber to build a haypress. He took a wagon to Conrad Kiel's (or Kyle) sawmill in the heavily timbered Charleston Mountains, thirty miles northwest of the ranch. Kiel ran a very primitive operation. The circular pacing of a solitary horse on top of a box structure sunk in a deep pit provided power to drive a gear that moved a large blade, cutting logs placed on a bench in the pit.

Delivery of a timber to the mill was even more crude. After a tree was felled, limbs were removed on the spot. Kiel wrapped a rope around the log several times, and the log rolled toward the mill as another horse uncoiled the line.

June 1   Lowe *by Alie* Tobacco   1.00

" 1   Clark & Moue on *cañon* Retter from   7.90

" 1   Hi Huntington 1 Large Bot Wine 75

" "   750 Hay by Lowe   7.50

" "   Herman at Ivanpah Assay   4.00

May 24"   " Huntington 1585 Hay

June 9   Southwestern M Co *by S.M.P 445* 462 Beef

" 10   McGuity to *by other man* posturage 1 mo/th 2.00

June 1st   C. Bennett 1200 Hay   12.00

" 8   " " by crocker 4m   2.00

" 8   S.W. M co *by charly B's man* to Posturage   3.00

" 1   " " " by Teamster Barney *on trip for Pioche* 6.00

" 14th   " " " 10 Blo 1765 — *1 Bale to crown*

July 8th   S.W. Co by Barney to posturage 2.00 2.00 *on one Horse of Shamrod & lucky*

June 20th   G. Allen two & weeks Board ~~14.00~~ 7.00

Settled *one Gass 161.53 Paid*

July 21   Settled in full with S.W.M Co

" 22   Mr Lowe 2 Large Plugs tobacco 2.00

" 22   Mr Blick coons Tobacco 4 1.00

July 1st   Herman Assay at Silver Reef 3.00

July 22   Settled in full with H. Myer came out Even *to A. Fisl* *by ~~Huntington~~ & cunningham & stein*

Aug 20   H. Myer posturage on 3 Animals 6.00

June 15   by Huff Tobacco 2.00

   Matches .50

   Tobacco 2.00

   Matches .50

This and the following two pages are leaves from O. D. Gass' day book. For about five years before 1881 he astutely observed the weather, recording temperatures and windy days. It snowed on the ranch in 1879. On this page business transactions and wages are paid. On the page following he notes his tax bill in 1877. On the third page the weight of his children are designated by initials. It is clearly evident that many of Gass' grapes made their way into wine barrels.

   1240 Hay 25 *Ra.ts* 12.40

27"   Beets .50

   corn Beef 1.50

Nov 11th   Finished Hauling Alfalfa

Alfalfa   lost time

     Finished Hauling Beans

Beans   to Bean Hulls to Fodder

     Made a general cleaning

     up of crops in good health

     although strong appearance

Grapes   of Rain. Foddered crops

Herds   Butter commenced

12th	Grapes	
12	Sue Bend?	$1.00
12	Sue Johston	1.21
13th	O. S. Gass left for California	
	to get coin for Mortgage	

1877
Nov
22   O. S. G Returned from cal with

     Bullion and paid mortgage

22   Cloudy and Rainy

22   ice   icicles 6 in long on trough

22   Niped Grapes very little & Peaches

     cut upper Ranch very Bad

23   warmer but windy cloudy

24   " " " "

25   " "

26   " "

27   " "

28   Assessor Here

29   Warm & Calm & pleasant   Mr Wines here

29   C Almendinger & Capt Swigler went

     Prospecting in Goss Mts

30th   cloudy Windy

Tax   Personal Property   23,85,00

"   Real Estate   3500.00

"   Total ---- 5 885 00

         3.50 per Hundred

     total Tax   223.60

Day	Temp	Temp 2	Category	Notes
1			Beans	Beans commenced to Blossom
2				
3				
4	102		Grapes	Commenced drying Grapes
5	104		Wine	commenced making Wine
6	102		"	finished drying "
7	100	58		Cold Nights
8	101	56		"
9	101	56		" "
10	106	60		Strong South wind
11	100	60		Lightning in the South — S. gall
12	100	61		, , ,
13	98	59		, , ,
14	75	58		clear culm
15	88	58		" "
16	100	60		, ,
17	92	60		, ,
18	92	65	Wine	finished making Wine
19	100	65		
20	92	70	Rain	clouded in morning & Rained Heavy at Rancho Cattle arrived in Vegas wash But continued on to colorado River at mouth of vegas wash
21	74	60	Colorado R	C S and family went to pence cattle and pu vejas wash
22	96	65		O. D. & Family arrived from colorado River a
23	100	70		
24	100	70		all in excellent Health
25	98	68	children	Weighed Jip 23 P—23 Fint 33 Le 36
26	95	75		
27	100	80		
28	100	80		
29	100	70		Changeable
30	18	75		Beans Ripening fast
				Commenced cur

Conrad Kiel was not a mountain man; he and his son, Ed, lived in a little two-room cabin on a small ranch two miles northwest of Gass. During the 1870's "Old Man" Kiel, a capable carpenter, built a water wheel in the stream just above the Gass ranch house. A flume carried water to the wheel which powered a grinding apparatus for grain, oats and barley. Men brought grain to the grinder in a wheel barrow.

Business trips from the ranch to his former El Dorado Canyon home concerned meat and vegetable deliveries to the Southwestern Mining Company based there. Corned beef was carried in heavy brine, and butter in big barrels. Trips were also taken to the Colorado River, to St. Thomas, Ivanpah in California, Pahranagat Valley, St. George and Silver Reef (both in Utah).

Though Gass knew the deserts, he had buried a few men who perished for lack of water. He offered travel advice to readers of the San Bernadino *Guardian:*

> Never travel alone; have a large canteen; rest before crossing the desert; feed your animal on all occasions where you can get supplies. If you have no means to do this, don't start until you have, as your life is at stake; drink, gorge yourself with water before starting to cross a desert, like an Indian; then keep cool; don't get scared and imagine yourself thirsty the first five miles and commence to gorge your water before you really need any. Ever remember that your life is in your canteen; draw it out with a zealous eye. . . . Never play with the Indians, like some rattle-brained boy and show them your guns, etc., as many have forfeited their lives for this imprudence. Never give Indians any species of ammunition or fire arms; you not only jeopardize your own life, but that of those who may come along after you. Any one who will thus supply them should be branded a coward and murderer. If the wild man of the forest should forget propriety enough to beg, give him a biscuit and a little tobacco. If he still begs, make him "git," and inform him of the beauties of self reliance—and stick to it.

> N. B. Invariably [before beginning your travels] get full directions about location of water, which side of the road, etc. etc. Never leave a plain wagon road in search of water (as some have done), thinking vainly that they knew more about water than a road. All wagon roads lead to springs and creeks. If you cannot follow these directions, "stay at home with the gal you love so much" and drink lager beer mit the dutch.

Legislator

In all, Gass served four consecutive terms in the Arizona Territorial legislature, from 1865 until 1868. During each session, which lasted about two months, a company of men continued to develop Las Vegas Ranch. During his first winter away four cattle had been stolen. Though some ranchers had used the bullwhip to frighten and punish some of the local troublemakers, other Indians continued to steal stock from various ranchers.

Even as a freshman O.D. Gass distinguished himself as a lawmaker. His interest in northwestern Arizona's development soon earned him the title of "Champion of the Upper Colorado." He helped draft the bill to create Pah-Ute County on December 22, 1865 out of Mohave County which until that date had covered all of the northwest corner of Arizona. The new entity embraced generally what is now Clark County, Nevada, and included Las Vegas, the Mormon Muddy River settlements and Callville, the county seat.

Five voters comprised the electorate at Las Vegas Precinct, Lincoln County, in 1870. Exactly a century later Las Vegas and adjacent North Las Vegas had 250 precincts and 57,854 voters. A set of 1970 voter affidavits weighs a little more than a half ton.

No.	DATE OF REGISTRY.	NAME OF ELECTOR.	AGE.	WHERE BORN.
1	Oct 16th	N. S. Lewis	41	Indiana
2	" 16th	James B. Wilson	44	Ohio
3	" 16	William Knapp	32	New York
4	" 16	S N Cole	37	Ohio
5	" 16	O. D. Gass	43	Ohio

50

In the latter community Gass had unbounded faith, "soon to be the largest city in Arizona," according to his letter early in 1866 to a friend in Prescott, where he mingled with other lawmakers. "From this point (Callville) the whole Utah trade will be supplied, also the southern part of Nevada." Months later he rejoiced when the first sternwheel steamboat, the *Esmeralda,* arrived in port at Callville early in the fall of 1866.

During the 1866 session that convened at Prescott on October 3, Gass represented the new Pah-Ute County in the upper chamber, the council. He had been elected without opposition. In that same session he was translator and interpreter. Though rough in speech, his contemporaries described him as very able: "He is a ranchman living at Callville; a man of quick wit, and more than usual intelligence. Although on intimate terms with the Mormons, we believe he is yet without a wife...."

This source among others lists Gass as a Callville resident, though no proof exists that he ever resided there. Callville was the nearest post office to Las Vegas Ranch. Even when postmaster of Callville from October 1867 to June 1869, Gass lived at the ranch. Another partner, James Ferry, actually handled the Callville mail and delivered it seventy miles downstream to and from Hardyville, a settlement on a regular east-west mail route.

After the roll call opened the 1867 session, the council honored Gass by electing him Presiding Officer. As Chairman of the important Military and Indian Affairs Committee, he noted deficiencies in Arizona Territorial military forces and tried to arrange for increased garrisons. In the spring of 1867 Gass asked the commanding officer at nearby Camp El Dorado to station troops at Las Vegas Ranch to protect Pah-Ute County from Indian robbers and marauders and watch over travelers on the Salt Lake trail.

This became a reality in May when a detachment of less than a dozen infantry arrived at Las Vegas Ranch. The men occupied a large adobe building with a high mud roof—very likely the one "fort" building still on the site in 1971. Fears of depredations soon proved to be unfounded, and in May 1869 the last of the troops left Las Vegas.

Probably the most important legislative item that passed the council under Gass' leadership was Territorial capital removal from Prescott southward to Tucson. Every southern Arizona councilman favored the move, while the north voted against it except for Gass. His "aye" provided the victory margin.

Prescott's citizens and especially the *Miner* editor gnashed their teeth when the bill became law. The editor asked, "What induced honorables O.D. Gass and R.J. Cutler of the Pah-Ute County to vote for removal? Was it the *silvery* eloquence of the men from Tucson, or their *greenness.* Probably both."

Other legislation guided by Gass included the transfer of the Pah-Ute County seat from Callville to St. Thomas, but the move proved to be futile. Several months earlier, in May 1866, Congress had passed an act that enabled the State of Nevada to acquire most of Pah-Ute County and every important town.

Immediately Gass joined other Arizona legislators in contesting the transfer, but a memorial to Congress asking for a recision fell on deaf ears. Arizonans argued correctly that there was no natural connection between Nevada's older settled portion and Pah-Ute County and that commerce in the transferred territory naturally flowed to the rest of Arizona.

Finally in January 1867 the Nevada legislature passed a resolution accepting the additional territory. Nevada thereafter had legal right to the land, though the section of the Nevada constitution describing the state boundaries was not amended at the same time to include the new area. Even more than a century later, the description of Nevada's boundaries in section fourteen of its constitution does not include the Las Vegas area. In modern times a few convicts have appealed to other bodies to declare their cases a mistrial, claiming that Las Vegas is still part of Arizona!

Though Gass' ranch was thereafter in Nevada, Arizona maintained *de facto* control for at least three more years. Despite the land transfer Pah-Ute County sent councilman Gass and assemblyman Andrew Gibbons to the territorial legislature in 1868. Even though the lawmakers appeared to be concerned with Pah-Ute's welfare, the land transfer could not be reversed.

To attend the legislative sessions at Tucson, the two men may well have made the most improbable and arduous journey that lawmakers ever took in the performance of their duty. On the first day of November, Gass and Gibbons left Callville in a homemade fourteen-foot rowboat and paddled and floated more than 300 miles down the Colorado River to Yuma in southwestern Arizona. Since Indian trouble discouraged all direct land travel, the river served as an expeditious alternate route.

PAH-UTE COUNTY

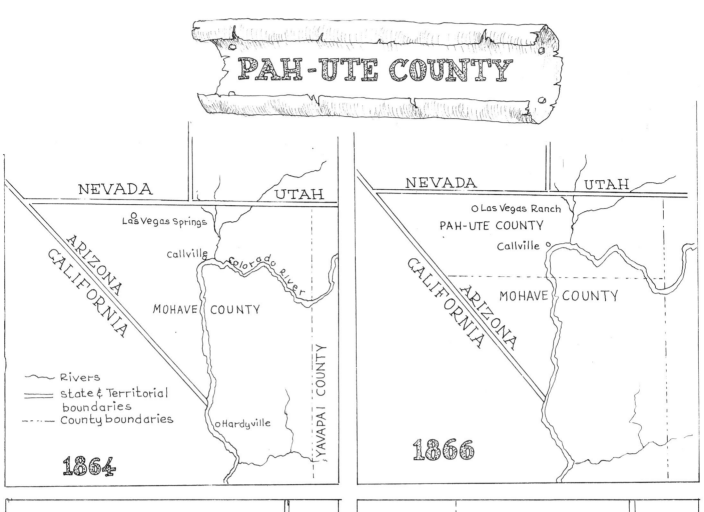

NEVADA   UTAH

o Las Vegas Springs

Callville

Colorado river

ARIZONA

CALIFORNIA

MOHAVE COUNTY

YAVAPAI COUNTY

~ Rivers
— State & Territorial boundaries
-·- County boundaries

o Hardyville

1864

NEVADA   UTAH

o Las Vegas Ranch

PAH-UTE COUNTY

Callville o

ARIZONA

CALIFORNIA

MOHAVE COUNTY

1866

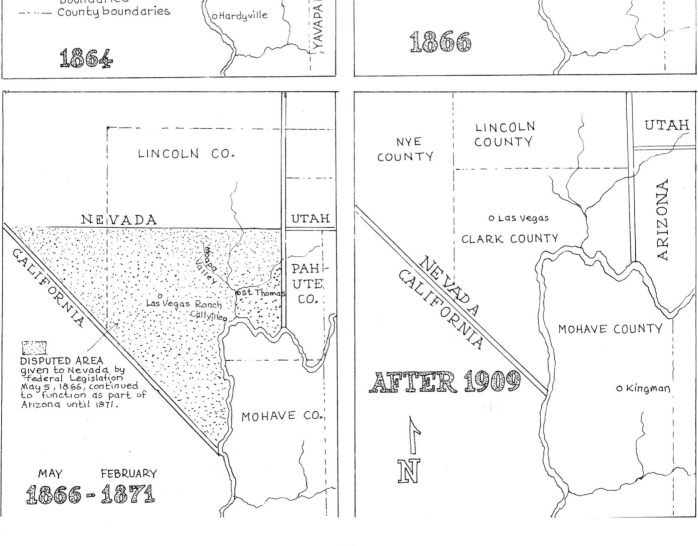

LINCOLN CO.

NEVADA   UTAH

Moapa Valley

PAH-UTE CO.

Las Vegas Ranch
Callville o

ost Thomas

CALIFORNIA

DISPUTED AREA given to Nevada by federal Legislation May 5, 1866, continued to function as part of Arizona until 1871.

MOHAVE CO.

MAY   FEBRUARY
1866 - 1871

NYE COUNTY

LINCOLN COUNTY

UTAH

o Las Vegas

CLARK COUNTY

ARIZONA

NEVADA

CALIFORNIA

AFTER 1909

MOHAVE COUNTY

o Kingman

N

In Black Canyon, the present location of Hoover Dam, as well as in other places, the river leaped and swirled wildly between the rugged canyon walls. The frightening roar of water and the perpendicular canyon walls extending several hundred feet above the water heightened the impression of drifting into eternity. Gibbons' reminiscences mention that Gass, who knew nothing about boating, merely stayed at the boat stern and closed his eyes when they encountered the crest of rapids.

From Yuma the two men planned to catch a stage for Tucson, but none was available because Apaches had recently killed the regular driver. Already late for the opening session, Gass and Gibbons after a short delay arrived at Tucson by coach in mid-November, about a week after the legislature had begun to grind out new laws. Gass, past his zenith as an innovative lawmaker, did nothing of importance in that 1868 session.

Earlier that same year Gass had tried to sell the ranch. In April 1868 he advertised in the St. George, Utah *Our Dixie Times* that he was making available twenty-acre parcels of $200 each. "The soil is a black rich loam and will produce vegetables or grain in abundance for markets down the Colorado, at El Dorado Canyon, Mohave City, Aubrey City and etc. There is water sufficient for about 400 acres of small grain and range for about 3000 head of stock. For particulars apply to O.D. Gass, Los Vegas, Arizona."

He did not dispose of his property. In 1870 another political consequence affected the former legislator. When a boundary survey finally determined that the Mormon settlements on the Muddy River belonged to Nevada's Lincoln County instead of Utah's Rio Virgin County, the former initiated tax suits to collect two years of taxes from the settlers.

Gass announced that he would contest Nevada's right to collect back taxes. His Mormon friends attempted to raise enough money to pay expenses to Carson City to lobby for a relief bill, but Gass probably did not make the trip. Rather than live in an unsympathetic state which might even someday interfere with their religion, the Mormons returned virtually *en-masse* to Utah early in 1871. A few Mormons remained with Protestants such as Gass. The Lincoln County sheriff plastered tax notices on abandoned buildings and fields were laid waste along the Muddy River.

The Arizona *Miner* had the last laugh: "The people of Prescott will hardly pity O.D. Gass if he is taxed upon his illy gotten money that was paid for his vote in removing the [Arizona] capital from Prescott to Tucson." Gass and others at the ranch had to pay more than $400 in taxes.

Justice of the Peace

Lincoln County records of the early 1870's list O.D. Gass as Justice of the Peace. One of the family legends concerns "O.D." when he held court in one of his ranch buildings. There had been a shooting scrape nearby involving one of the local Paiutes. Evidence was assembled and witnesses present, but Gass faced a dilemma. A reaction from the local Paiutes would follow whether Gass punished or freed the prisoner.

So when noon arrived Gass left an armed Indian to guard the accused. While Gass and the others dined in the main ranch house a shot rang out. The prisoner had tried to escape, but the guard after being knocked down recovered his gun and shot the fleeing Indian. That closed the case and Gass did not have to pass judgment. Gass believed that the prisoner would try to run away and thus he left an Indian guard.

Other killings occurred at the ranch in the late 1860's. In the fall of 1867 while Gass was legislating at Prescott, a man named Mooney shot two men in the chest at St. Thomas. Then without provisions or even a canteen he vaulted into a saddle and fled across fifty-five miles of waterless desert to Las Vegas. Three horsemen followed in hot pursuit.

Arriving at the ranch, the exhausted Mooney dashed for the stream near the ranch house and flung himself into the water. He drank deeply, dunked his head and hands to revive himself and then ran about 200 yards east into a mesquite thicket. His pursuers arrived only fifteen minutes later, nearly perishing because of a lack of water, as they also had set out hastily without canteens. They ignored the stream, pressing their search for Mooney. Soon they flushed him out of hiding and forced him to fire at them. Returning the fire, one of the pursuers shot Mooney in the heart. He was buried where he fell beside a gnarled mesquite tree on the flat below the ranch house.

Another incident that took place on a hot July day in 1868 involved the local detachment of army soldiers. An afternoon of wine drinking to relieve the tedium of desert garrison duty climaxed with the killing of Private Barron after he exchanged hot words with Private Connelly. The two men had quarreled in a mud hut, and after Barron allegedly bit Connelly in the face, the latter responded with his gun. The other men gave vague testimony

Mary Virginia Simpson Gass (1841-1925) was the daughter of a wealthy Missouri farmer. Her black eyes accented her fair skin and wavy waist-length brunette hair. She was considered unusually tall at five feet, eight inches, with a slender figure.

because all were filled with wine. Since Barron was not killed in the line of duty, Connelly was to be turned over to California civilian authorities for trial, but he deserted and never was found.

Family Life

During the winter of 1871 a young Missourian of fair complexion and dark hair, Mary Virginia Simpson, traveled west on the transcontinental train with the children of her sister, Ann Jennings. In Ogden, Utah, they were met by her sister and her new husband, who had a small caravan of covered wagons to take them over the trail southward through Las Vegas to Arizona.

While driving a wagon hitched to a four-mule team through southwestern Utah, Miss Simpson according to Gass family tradition, met an important western leader. A galloping horseman approaching from the opposite direction waved his hands wildly and shouted to her and the others,

"Get out of the road, get out of the road! The President is a comin'!"

Miss Simpson inquired, "Who is the President?"

"Why Brigham Young! Now out of the way!"

"Well, he can have half of the road, and the other half is mine."

And as they passed each other Young yielded half of the road, and while tipping his hat he bid her "good-day."

The caravan stopped at Las Vegas Ranch to repair wagons and rest before hurrying on farther south. Because of difficulties in crossing the Colorado River, Miss Simpson and the Jennings family went to Moapa Valley where they were able to purchase at a low price a farm from one of the Mormons who wanted to return to Utah in February 1871. Miss Simpson then went to live with her sister's family at St. Thomas.

After courting by many sixty-mile buckboard journeys and horseback rides, Gass married her at Pioche on February 24, 1872. They eventually had four boys and three girls. Among the six born while they lived at the ranch, two died in infancy. One boy was born later in California.

Mrs. Gass was distinctly domestic. Though Indian women did the washing and cleaning, and a Chinese the cooking, she made such garments as sleeveless vests, socks, caps and dresses. She also taught the Indians how to do that work for themselves. She sewed with her left hand, though she did many things well with either. With a single barrel shotgun she occasionally gunned down chicken hawks that flew near the main ranch buildings. Because of this the Indians called her "long eye" or "sharp eye."

The children respected their mother and thus she seldom had to punish them. While leaving the house to hunt or play, they were usually instructed to return by sundown. They ran a mile to obey her. In the warm summer nights she prepared the beds on a porch outside the house where croaking frogs and the chirps of crickets sang them to sleep.

Gass was not too busy to play with his children. The oldest daughter, Lelah Vegas, enjoyed riding on the mowing machine with her father when he cut the alfalfa. At night he taught the children astronomy and told them stories until they fell asleep.

Gass' children played hide and seek, tag and other games with the Wilson, Knapp and the Indian children. All liked to watch geese land in a small swamp inside the pasture or run with their dogs.

They also enjoyed horseback, but Gass insisted that they always ask the foreman's permission before taking a horse away from the stables.

Occasionally the boys invented mischief. Early one day, prospectors who had camped inside the stockade cooked breakfast over a campfire before moving on, leaving burning embers. One of the boys playing in the area picked up a lighted stick, climbed on top of a haystack along the stockade's east side, and stuck the burning wood into the straw. Fortunately, the foreman quickly doused the fire with water. He scolded the boy by promising a spanking if he played with fire again. When the boy snapped back, the foreman cuffed him on the ear and ordered him to the house. On the way back, the boy spotted a tin can and threw it at the foreman, cutting him on the nose. The boy received a spanking that he never forgot for the rest of his life.

Holidays on the ranch were special occasions. The Fourth of July began at about sunrise with the shooting of the anvils, a common western custom. Other men fired their guns in a salute when a flag was raised in the dry breeze. Later in the day a chicken and wine dinner capped the festivities. Afterwards the men pitched horseshoes and sipped wine.

Before each Christmas a few of the hands would ride to the mountains to get a tree tall enough to reach the ceiling of the main ranch house. Until Christmas Day a sheet was suspended in front of the tree. Useful and comic objects adorned it. Gifts would be distributed and there was always something for everybody, including the Indians. The children usually received small gifts including wooden pails filled with hard candy brought in from San Bernardino. They always looked forward to the packages which came from the Jennings family in St. Thomas and from Mrs. Gass' parents in Missouri. The immediate family enjoyed a chicken or roast with pie and cake on Christmas Day.

The family spent most of their evenings together both while living at the ranch and later after moving to California. After eating, favorite pastimes were playing dominoes and reading. By kerosene lamp Lelah Vegas would read to her brothers and sisters a couple of chapters about Stanley and Livingstone or the big game hunters in Africa. The family retired early, using candles to light the room until they were in bed.

In 1880 Gass traveled to the Pomona area to look for a new home. Two children were old enough to attend school, and there was none at

Las Vegas. Bad weather had destroyed some recent crops. Most important of all a burdensome mortgage with an interest rate of 2½% per month forced Gass to leave his home of fifteen years.

Gass had initially mortgaged his property to neighbor William Knapp in 1874 for $3000. This was paid back in time after Gass made a trip to California to get bullion. In August 1879 he borrowed $5000 in gold coin from rancher Archibald Stewart of Bristol, north of Pioche. The promissory note secured by a mortgage on the 640-acre Las Vegas Ranch and the 160-acre Spring Ranch, was to be paid back in a year's time. This amounted to purchasing the ranch because exactly a year later Gass could not repay and Stewart acquired all of Gass' property for $6,478.

O.D. Gass — Later Years

When the Gass family left the ranch in June, 1881, they traveled for three weeks with a small herd of cattle to a ranch about ten miles south of Pomona. He stayed there briefly but soon moved to start a farm about halfway between San Bernardino and Colton. He also attempted to raise early grapes at Caliente Hot Springs, but strong winds and poor water control scuttled the effort. Voting records give Gass' occupation as farmer through 1884.

By the fall of 1885 the mining fever had caught Gass again. That year he joined prospecting parties which explored Lower California and the wilds of eastern San Bernardino County. All ventures were unsuccessful, and times were not good for the Gass family. Voting rolls list Gass' occupation as miner beginning in 1888.

Just after 1900 this grey-eyed citizen of the Southwest, with flowing white hair, moved to the home of his son, Fenton, in Bryn Mawr, near Redlands, California. Until his death on December 10, 1924, O.D. Gass tended a small garden and helped with light chores around his son's orange groves. Burial was in the Masonic Plot of the Hillside Cemetery in Redlands.

Las Vegas Ranch After Gass

Early in the summer of 1881, after the Gass family left Nevada, the ranch did not remain vacant. That same summer Stewart sold a third interest in the ranch properties to George Hagerty who moved there to take charge of the operations. Hagerty made great improvements in the property, including opening a small store for travelers. From that year's grape crop 600 gallons of wine were made and about a ton of raisins cured.

In about 1885 Gass (left) and his closest friend F. M. Slaughter, a native of Missouri, posed for this picture in a Los Angeles studio. These men of a quiet disposition initially met on California's Mother Lode in the early 1850's. Each named children after one another, and Gass' eldest daughter, Lelah Vegas, married Slaughter's son, further cementing the relationship between the families. Gass always wore a long, curly ten-inch brown beard which was slightly darker than his wavy hair. His long dark colored frock coat contrasts with his smartly tailored tweed trousers that extend over his polished boots. A heavy gold chain is attached to an ornate watch in his vest pocket.

Slaughter's light suit has a velvet collar. For more than twenty years he maintained a successful farm near Chino, California, while Gass on the other hand farmed at Las Vegas and mined for gold and silver in the deserts along the Colorado River.

In April 1882 Archie Stewart took his family to Las Vegas Ranch to manage the operation in place of Hagerty. Two months later a California party reportedly tried to purchase the ranch for $11,000 but Stewart refused to sell.

When Stewart arrived at his ranch, Conrad Kiel still owned a ranch two miles to the northwest. Two years later, in the summer of 1884, Stewart was killed there in a controversial shooting. Three written sources agree that a Las Vegas ranch employee named Henry shot Stewart near the main ranch house of the Kiel Ranch, though details have been lost amid a maze of apocryphal stories.

An initial report stated that notorious area "bad man" Hank Parrish did the killing. Only three years earlier that El Dorado Canyon miner had been involved in a shooting affray in an intense all-night poker game with two other miners. One of the victims held four jacks while Parrish bet heavily on aces full on kings.

Parrish left the game but returned a few minutes later with a pistol in each hand and began shooting at the players. One of them received deep wounds in the chest and abdomen. No attempt was made to arrest Parrish. A few hours later he went to the wounded man to obtain $100 in gambling losses. After securing it he returned to the mines, but the wounded man died before he could secure medical help. The other player was crippled for life.

The sheriff did not arrest Parrish because the Commissioners thought that trial expenses would be too large for the near-bankrupt county. The reputation of Parrish as a desperado grew, and he was accused of killing many people including Stewart. Finally in 1890 a grand jury investigated Parrish for murdering a miner near Pioche. The indictment concluded that he was "guilty of a cold blooded dastardly murder, one for which his neck should stretch in punishment."

Prior to Stewart's death, he and Henry had quarreled for many days. While his boss was away in El Dorado Canyon, Henry walked off the job. After returning home and learning that Henry was at Kiel's, Stewart grabbed a rifle under the pretense of going to kill a steer. Instead, he remounted his horse and after taking a circuitous route he entered the Kiel Ranch on the north side. He hitched his horse to a tree hidden behind a cluster of grapevines and crept toward the house.

When Stewart was only about ten yards from the ranch house, Henry saw the aggressor with his gun aimed at the house windows. All of them were wide open and Henry was sitting inside. He grabbed a gun to defend himself, but thinking that it was unloaded he tossed it aside. Henry then sprang across the room and took a Spencer rifle from the scabbard. Stewart saw him move and fired but missed. Henry unsuccessfuly returned the fire. Seeing that Stewart was getting ready to shoot again, Henry stepped behind the main ranch house door. His adversary placed his gun barrel against the door and fired, and the bullet grazed Henry's arm.

By then Henry had time to reload. He stepped from behind the door and both men fired. Though hit in the leg, Henry was able to shoot Stewart in the chest. After another exchange of fire Stewart was felled with a bullet in the skull. Not a word was spoken during the encounter.

Everyone in the area believed that Henry killed in self-defense. Not much sympathy was expressed for Stewart, and many believed that he was an overbearing man who had met his just desserts.

Kiel was away at the time of the shooting. When he returned he wrote a terse note to Mrs. Stewart: "Your husband is here dead. Come take him away." At the murder scene she found the body outside of the house and covered with a blanket. His beard had been burned, and a facial wound led her to conclude that more than one man was involved in the killing.

Mrs. Helen J. Stewart continued to live at Las Vegas Ranch until early in this century. A foreman directed the ranching and farm activities. The ranch became a sort of resort for southern Nevada prospectors and miners who welcomed a change from biscuits, jerky and flapjacks. At the ranch they had shade, milk and good beef to eat on a clean table. She charged about a dollar a day for board, and the men slept under the big trees on the ranch.

In the last century other important southern Nevada desert ranches were at Indian Springs, forty miles northwest of Las Vegas and in Pahrump Valley, sixty miles west. There the Pahrump Ranch was overshadowed in importance by the extensive Manse Ranch which was started by Joseph Yount in 1876. Around 1900 the Manse had more than 160 acres of fruit orchards and gardens under cultivation. In Las Vegas Valley the Kiel Ranch later was known as the Park Ranch, the Taylor Ranch, Boulderado, and finally the Losee Ranch.

At the turn of the century Las Vegas Ranch was a notable example of desert fertility and productiveness, made possible by extensive irrigation and water diversion from Las Vegas Creek, shown in the foreground of the bottom picture. The main ranch house is behind the fashionably dressed women seated on a fallen log. This prospector's retreat had many residents, especially during the weeks before Las Vegas townsite was auctioned on May 15, 1905. The site is along the east side of Las Vegas Boulevard North, below the modern Elks Club. Burros (above) were not an uncommon sight on ranch property.

The dining room and doorway of the main ranch house are shown here as they were in 1907. On the mantle in the dining room is part of Mrs. Helen J. Stewart's fine collection of baskets made by Las Vegas Paiute Indians.

Ranking second in importance among area ranches after Las Vegas Ranch was the nearby Kyle (Kiel) Ranch in the modern North Las Vegas area. After 1905 it supplied Las Vegas markets with fruits and vegetables, especially luscious apricots, sweet black figs, early yellow apples with a fine flavor, and all sorts of garden vegetable products including beets, carrots and turnips. The valley's first artesian well was drilled there, and the land became productive at the touch of water.

Below, hay is being mowed and hauled away. Pork was also an important product. On the opposite page with the camera pointed north, the main ranch house built by John S. Park is shown at the edge of a long poplar-shaded driveway and walkway. Immediately behind the house is an older building which dates before 1890 when Archibald Stewart was killed there (see text). The ranch has been the scene of many other desert tragedies. For some time up to October 1900 bachelor brothers Edward and William Kyle had quarreled. The former shot the latter and then committed suicide. A few Indians still wearing their moccasins also are buried on the premises.

At the base of Red Rock Canyon, 25 miles southwest of Las Vegas, was the Wilson or Sandstone Ranch, established about 1880 by James B. Wilson. Its founder was a squaw man who in the 1870's delivered beef in the cool of the night from Las Vegas Ranch to El Dorado Canyon. He died in 1906, leaving the property to his two sons Jim and Tweed Wilson. Some of its modern glamorous owners were Chet Lauck, the "Lum" of "Lum and Abner" radio fame; Mrs. Vera Krupp, German munitions heiress from whom a half million dollar diamond was stolen there (it was returned later); and billionaire Howard Hughes. Lauck built a luxurious house in the shadow of these colorful cliffs. But the Wilson homestead cabin shown here remained the home of the Wilson brothers until their deaths. This was thoughtfully provided in a deed made by Mrs. George Fayle, owner of the Ranch in the 1920's.

"As a resort, the Manse had no equal in Southern Nevada," an old prospector once said. With a delightful climate the Manse Ranch, sixty miles west of Las Vegas behind the Spring Mountain Range, was a good place to rest after a season of searching for minerals in the nearby mountains. Excellent accommodations for both man and beast were at this oasis, made possible by natural springs. Fresh beef was available nearly every week for ranchhands and teamsters alike, who stopped here on the Ivanpah-Bullfrog freight runs. Another aspect of the Manse was a sawmill operation on the west flank of the Spring Mountains in Clark Canyon. Freshly cut timber was delivered to Bullfrog before the completion of a railroad between Las Vegas and the mining camp in 1906.

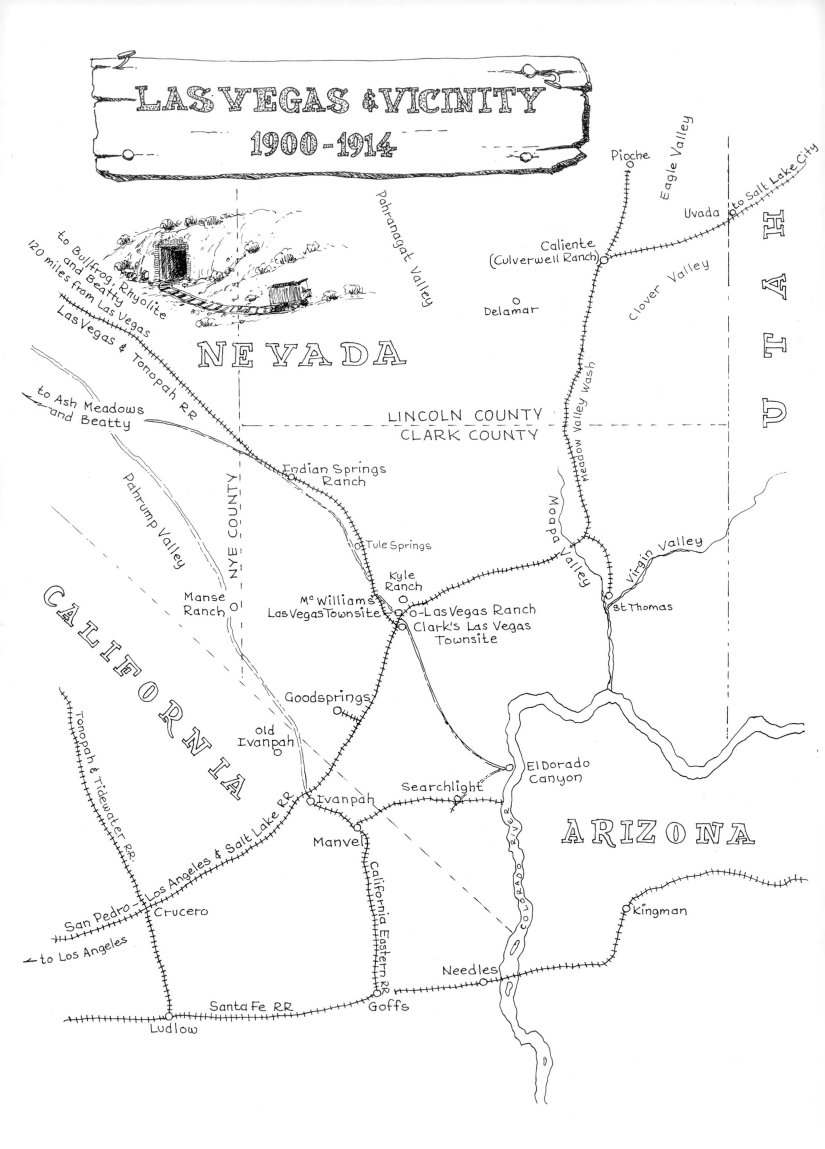

CHAPTER FIVE

The Founding of Las Vegas

SOUTHERN NEVADA'S LARGEST TOWN IN 1900 WAS DELAmar, a booming gold mining camp of 1000 people, located about a hundred miles directly north of Las Vegas. It was larger than Pioche, a silver mining camp which had seen its best days in the 1870's. The other large town in southern Nevada was Searchlight, sixty miles south of Las Vegas, which was emerging as a promising gold mining camp. Extensive farms and ranches were in Eagle, Clover, Moapa and Virgin Valleys, all near the Nevada-Utah border. At that time the entire Las Vegas Valley had only thirty residents.

No railroads crossed southern Nevada in 1900. Railheads were Manvel in eastern California and Uvada, Utah, a station close to the Nevada-Utah border on the Oregon Short Line (part of the Union Pacific system). Nevertheless, powerful railroad forces would soon disturb the serenity of Las Vegas Valley, bringing about the founding of Las Vegas as a town in 1905.

In 1899 the Oregon Short line had organized another company to build into Nevada and California. Then in August 1900 Montana Senator William Clark formed a competitive line, soon to be known as the San Pedro, Los Angeles & Salt Lake Railroad, which would traverse the same territory.

An immediate dispute raged over an abandoned railroad grade extending eastward from Culverwell Ranch (Caliente) toward Uvada. Each line claimed to own valid documents and old surveys. In April 1901, while awaiting a court decision concerning the right of way, each contender sent armies of men to perfect the grade. On one occasion physical violence erupted involving an angry exchange of blows with both shovels and fists. Moreover, the two competing companies disputed the right to cross Culverwell Ranch, and each side hastily prepared a grade through treacherous Meadow Valley Wash, south from Caliente in the direction of Las Vegas.

Both rivals eyed choice sites in Las Vegas Valley as a natural division point for shop facilities and a town, because of a plentiful water supply and the availability of timber standing on nearby mountains. In the valley's midst was Mrs. Helen J. Stewart's Las Vegas Ranch with 1800 to 2000 fenced acres. Figs, dates and tropical fruits grew in a fine orchard sustained by 400 inches of water diverted from Las Vegas creek for irrigation.

In June 1901 the Oregon Short Line leaped into action first to obtain the ranch land and water supply by securing an option to purchase both for $60,000. It forfeited those rights. After the O.S.L. and the S.P., L.A. & S.L. made a truce in the summer of 1902, the latter company under Senator Clark paid $55,000 for the ranch and springs. Only $5000 secured it, and the balance was paid in December 1902. The Clark forces then vigorously pushed construction southward toward Las Vegas.

Building the railroad grade into Las Vegas Valley was underway in the summer heat of 1904. As construction progressed tent saloons, stores and boarding houses kept pace with the graders at the end of the track. Later in the summer a tent settlement called Las Vegas sprang up a half mile west of Las Vegas Ranch. Steel rails reached near there on October 20, 1904, and eastward connection with scheduled through service was a reality by the end of that month.

In preparation for the building of the San Pedro, Los Angeles & Salt Lake Railroad early in this century, the railroad sent surveying parties into the southern Nevada wilderness. Surveyors traveled in spring wagons and made camp near tree-shaded streams and ponds, as shown above. From the left is William McDermott, William Matthews (the campmaster), Charles Whittemore, Judge Davis and Henry Lee. The setting is probably somewhere along Meadow Valley Wash in Lincoln County.

On the opposite page are views of the railroad surveyors in the Manvel, California area. Lee led the horses some distance from the railroad to water them at a desert well. In front of the buggy, Davis is flagging a train so that Whittemore (far left) and his luggage could return to Los Angeles over the Santa Fe Railroad, via Manvel.

66

Though the graders quickly moved southward this Las Vegas tent settlement thrived because here freight for the newly discovered Bullfrog mining district, 120 miles northwest near modern Beatty, was transferred onto wagons to begin the dusty trip in stagecoaches and freight wagons.

As the rush to Bullfrog intensified that fall, the helter-skelter transient settlement grew. Rounders, garroters and thieves mingled with teamsters, swampers, saloon men and railroad construction workers. By early November more than a dozen saloons and gambling houses were doing a rushing business. Alongside them were two meat markets, two stores and four restaurants housed under canvas and boards.

At Las Vegas Ranch was a post office in the charge of Walter Bracken, a meat market, a store, and a hotel where "ham-ands" were available for breakfast, and beefsteak, fried potatoes and coffee for supper. Near springs throughout the valley, small ranches produced a variety of fruit including apples and oranges, as well as almonds and sweet potatoes. Trees on the Kyle ranch bore prize winning figs. Wild grapes and gourds grew in profusion.

By November 1904 all kinds of speculation filled the air. One rumor had it that a large sanitorium would be built at Las Vegas. Others said that a lumber company might erect a sawmill west of Las Vegas Ranch and haul timber by railroad from the Spring Mountains. It was also thought that the excellent climate would allow luxuriant growth of tropic fruits, especially dates and figs in sufficient quantity to rival the most favored sections of southern California.

Early in 1905 the young town's businesses thrived because of the immense Bullfrog freight traffic. The tent town owner was a tall young red-headed engineer and surveyor named J.T. McWilliams, who initially had settled at Goodsprings in 1894. When Helen J. Stewart hired him in 1902 to survey the ranch boundaries in preparation for the sale to Clark's railroad company, McWilliams caught the Las Vegas fever.

This panorama looking south was taken very early in the fall of 1904 when construction was taking place through the north end of Las Vegas Valley. Wheeled scrapers drawn by two- to four-horse teams are shaping and leveling the sub-grade, using borrowed dirt from the area to the right. The workers sought refuge in the shade at the Kyle Ranch at right, where they mingled with prospectors (below) who came in to water their animals.

When through train service was initiated early in 1905 the Los Angeles Times editorialized: "It is hoped that the close connection that now exists with Salt Lake will not bring us into any undue familiarity with those plural marriage ideas. We have enough trouble as it is."

In 1904 Las Vegas post office operated in this humble structure.

He determined that an eighty acre government tract adjoined the ranch on the west and promptly filed on the land. After surveying a townsite called Las Vegas, he recorded his plat at the Lincoln County courthouse in Pioche. All of his streets and alleys were on the west side of the railroad tracks, although McWilliams also owned a quarter section east of the tracks because the rails had been laid mistakenly through the southeast corner of his acres. Through the winter of 1905 McWilliams sold land with a low down and liberal time payments.

The cluster of tents on his townsite was regarded as a good miner's supply point. In January 1905 a Goldfield miner wrote to his Los Angeles brother who wanted to move to the mineral fields. "I think the only thing to do is wait until the Clark road gets to running and then go to Vegas...and outfit there for your trip to Goldfield."

After Senator Clark announced that Las Vegas would be a division point on his line, materials by the carload arrived late in January to build dwellings, an ice plant, a roundhouse and shops. A Salt Lake City barber forwarded a bath tub, a chair and other equipment and opened for business by the first of February.

Las Vegas then contained about 150 buildings completed and under construction. An ice house 127 feet long by 55 feet wide was on the drawing boards. Two brickyards had contracts on hand to keep them busy for the next six months. Additional businesses started up, and hustle and bustle permeated the town. Everyone wondered where and when the railroad would lay out its townsite. Since McWilliams had already taken the name Las Vegas, what would it be called? No matter. The locals believed that their town, on the west side of the tracks and at the gate to Bullfrog and other northern mining camps, would be preferable to a town built on the east side of the tracks.

Finally on January 30, 1905 the San Pedro, Los Angeles & Salt Lake Railroad began running from California after connection had been made at a point twenty-three miles south of Las Vegas. A few days later the first train rumbled over the line all the way between the towns in the railroad's corporate name, though regular through service did not begin until May.

Charles "Pop" Squires was one of the first men to arrive in Las Vegas over the newly laid rails. The train on which he rode chuffed into Las Vegas Valley early in February, just as the glory of another day broke over Sunrise Mountain. Squires saw a conductor on the front platform and moved over to talk with him.

On the carpet of the pale green desert Squires noted a few tiny white specks which seemed about fifteen miles away but steadily growing larger.

"What is that?" he asked.

The conductor cleared his throat and spat vigorously. "That's Las Vegas," he replied.

As the train bumped along the white spots became better defined and then proved to be canvas buildings. Squires' train halted on a side track near an old passenger coach on which was nailed a board with "Las Vegas" painted on it.

After he stepped down from the caboose, he found himself surrounded by ugly clumps of desert brush. Just east of the right of way, he spotted a small tent where a Chinese was frying eggs and ham, and he decided to have breakfast. A few yards beyond, was a brightly lighted tent crudely marked "Ladd's Hotel." After eating he strolled through the canvas flaps of that place and stood in line at a rough board desk to register. A dollar entitled a person to sleep in a double bed with another stranger for an eight hour shift.

Squires warmed himself beside a pot-bellied stove. While thawing out he noted a young teamster entering the tent and asking for a bed. The hotel proprietor, Captain James H. Ladd, told him to be seated until one was ready. Since all beds were unoccupied Squires thought it unusual that the tired teamster, just in from Beatty after driving a sixteen-mule freight team, had to wait about a half hour before being allowed to sleep.

Later Squires learned that the proprietor wanted to see if the teamster would scratch—a sure sign that he carried bugs in his clothes and on his body. The stove's heat made a man itch if he were afflicted, and thus he would be unwelcome.

Other than these establishments, the railroad restricted anyone from camping on its land to avoid filling it with "sooners." New arrivals during February 1905 continued to buy land from McWilliams and settle on his Las Vegas townsite. He sold lots cheap, without promise of a water system or street improvements. Purchasers sank wells eight or ten feet and drew plenty of water.

These few hundred adventurous settlers, drawn together as if by some common purpose, had come from throughout the nation to seek easy wealth. Winter's hardships did not cloud their dreams. Occupations varied greatly, though saloon men and gamblers seemed to be predominant.

Railroad Street, a row of tents facing the tracks, and containing stores, a mercantile company, lodging houses and saloons, was a busy mart in southern Nevada's booming wonder town. The canvas hotels held no heat, and raw cold winds blew through them relentlessly. Tick mattresses filled with straw were laid on a frozen ground, and occupants had only one or two thin cotton blankets.

Men congregated in the warm tent saloons after sundown. Teamsters, miners, prospectors and cowpunchers in flannel shirts and overalls crowded around the tables. Each had tucked in his belt a roll of small bills with the ends hanging down as a fringe of security which no one dared violate. Within reach was a hidden gun.

During the long evenings men huddled near the stove and gulped occasional shots of whiskey while gambling. These pleasures, even if one were losing, were preferable to going to bed in the cold.

One of the teamsters, Captain Ray Gibson, spent many evenings in a wood-frame saloon which was about fifty feet long. A wooden bar extended the full length of the room on the left, and on the opposite side was a piano where a young musician played ragtime tunes. Plain-dressed railroad men, dusty prospectors and miners crowded around scattered tables playing cards while drinking strong whiskey and telling wild stories. A few women in gaudy satins danced with the men and induced them to drink at the bar to increase their commissions on the liquor sales.

A certain tall aged Englishman used to sit beside the piano when he was tight. His big ugly hands showed scars from long hard work as a boilermaker, yet Gibson perceived that he had a gentler history. He noticed that every time he heard a sour note, the old man cringed and dramatically clapped his hands over his ears. Gibson guessed that he knew good music.

And so when the regular player left briefly to make a trip to the outhouse, Gibson leaned toward the old man and asked, "Can you play that thing?"

"Sure."

"Well, get up there and play for us."

"The boy wouldn't like it."

"Get up there and play!"

Soon everybody stopped what they were doing and gathered around the old man to listen to compositions of Chopin, Mozart, and other classical greats, all being played in that dismal shanty in the midst of the Las Vegas desert.

When the regular player returned, he was astonished at what he heard. He begged the old man's pardon, for he used to say to him, "Get away from here, you old drunk!"

Gibson asked him where he had learned music.

In a deep rough voice the boilermaker replied, "Well, before John Barleycorn got me many years ago, I was a pianist in the court of Queen Victoria!"

Behind the business district immense well-fenced corrals held hundreds of horses and mules

In the spring of 1905 McWilliams' Las Vegas townsite boomed as a transportation center where goods and supplies brought in by railroad were transported to heavy freight wagons for delivery to area mining camps, especially Rhyolite in the Bullfrog district. After the Clark townsite opened later that spring, this town declined. Its rise and fall ranks among the speediest ever recorded in the annals of boom towns. In later years that area became "Westside" and finally "West Las Vegas"

Shown above is Bonanza (Clark) Avenue, abundantly lined with tents and shacks, with Sunrise (Frenchman) Mountain in the background. Freighters traversing this thoroughfare kicked up considerable dust which together with the heat made living uncomfortable. Local lumber merchant Jake Beckley (below), a partner of Ed Von Tobel, Sr., pauses beside his Bullfrog-bound wagon loaded with sacks of feed and lumber held in place by chains and jacks.

On the opposite page (top) other goods including hay and machinery are piled on larger wagons, while below are the wagon yards of the original Las Vegas. Wagons are being prepared for the dusty week-long trek to the Bullfrog district.

used by freighting concerns, though some animals belonged to railroad contractors. Many freighters headquartered in Las Vegas, providing profitable jobs for anyone who could crack a whip or punch a mule.

By March 1905 all the Los Angeles talk centered on how to capture the Las Vegas trade and speculation on the location of the permanent railroad depot. Late that same month railroad surveyors began driving stakes to mark lots in the long-awaited railroad townsite. The railroad also opened the Kuhn Mercantile store in a tent near present day Fremont and Main Streets. This was a block from the previously established Ladd Hotel near modern Main and Carson Streets.

Fortune also came to McWilliams in March 1905. When the railroad company engineers looked for a place to build its Armour ice plant, they chose a site on the east side of the tracks just north of modern Bonanza Avenue. After McWilliams saw where the surveyors had pounded their stakes he was shocked! Las Vegas' one great industry had been planned on his small triangle quarter-section east of the tracks.

Instantly McWilliams gained two advantages: his town would benefit greatly from the nearness of the new community industry, and he might be able to make the upstart railroad company pay exorbitantly for the ground. McWilliams decided to let the company dig foundation trenches and begin pouring concrete before calling the railroad company to account.

Late in March the press arrived. T.L. Reber began weekly publication of the *Times* on March 25, though James Brown assumed the editorship after two or three issues. It was described as "replete with local news." Every Saturday it was distributed from McWilliams' Las Vegas. Six days later, W.W. Wallace began to compete for subscribers and advertising by publishing the *Advance* every Friday. It was short-lived, probably folding late that same summer. The *Times,* however, continued weekly publication until late in the summer of 1906.

With establishment of still another weekly, the *Age,* on April 7, an editor at Pioche remarked that newspapers in Las Vegas Valley were as thick as townsites. At that time two new paper towns were being platted, and additions to McWilliams' town were being made. The Pioche editor suggested the propriety of consolidating all of them and calling it "Greater Las Vegas."

Early in April the railroad company announced that a contractor would soon start construction on a seventeen-stall roundhouse. Though work on it was off to a good start, by the month's end torrential rains softened the ground and filled excavations with water. Violent winds blew down the newly constructed brick walls.

That same month John S. Park opened the First State Bank of Las Vegas, although incorporation papers were not received until early in May. He transacted business behind two one-by-twelve inch boards thrown across the front of the Kuhn Company store, and behind him stood a big iron safe, the town's emblem of security. Cashier Park obtained it in Los Angeles, along with books and stationery. This was the town's second bank. Previously, in March, Los Angeles bankers with $100,000 in capital opened the Las Vegas Bank & Trust Company.

Also early in April, Salt Lake Railroad President J. Ross Clark, brother of Senator William Clark, announced that the railroad would officially open for through traffic on April 11, but he postponed the townsite lot sale until the first of May. Parcels would be sold at prices marked on the town plat, in the order that applications were received. Registrar Park accepted deposits at the bank, and for a few days business was brisk. People crowded near the crude desk to register their choices, and Park signed receipts for thousands of dollars.

Meanwhile, the famed Las Vegas Ranch was being transformed into a retreat for tired Las Vegans. Harry Beale managed the facilities which included a screened dining hall adjacent to the ranch house. It had windows on three sides with a spectacular view of Sunrise Mountain. On the south bank of Las Vegas Creek an open air pavilion could accommodate eight sets of quadrilles. A nearby brick store building contained the valley's only billiard table. Guests stayed in adobe buildings and newer tent houses, which had rates "no higher than one pays for a stuffy room in a commercial hotel in a smokey city." A swimming pool formed in the creek where it had been dammed, and patrons could rent bathing suits. Canvas walls enclosed part of the pool.

A grand ball and banquet opened the resort on April 30. Thereafter it was the scene of sylvan pleasure, where a Las Vegas businessman could in minutes lower his temperature and raise his spirits. The resort was nestled in the coziest nook of the entire valley, where only balmy breezes wafted when high desert winds blew nearby.

Las Vegas' first public swimming pool was at Las Vegas Ranch under huge cottonwood trees that shaded the headquarters area. To escape the summer heat, many early Las Vegas families spent the day here swimming or sitting in the shade eating a picnic lunch. Extensive orchards at Las Vegas Ranch included trees bearing apples, peaches, figs, apricots and almonds. Most of the trees were planted by O. D. Gass.

All during that spring the mining camps of Bullfrog and Rhyolite boomed tempestuously with increasing demands for materials and supplies. Large shipments out of Los Angeles arrived in Las Vegas daily, most of which were transferred to wagons for delivery to miners and merchants in the land of the Bullfrog. In one certain week Ed W. Clark's Wholesale Company received seven carloads of freight. Four contained lumber, two were mostly animal feed, and the other was filled with blasting powder and mining supplies.

Every general store did a lucrative business, especially in outfitting miners and prospectors who came into town with their burros to rest a few days before heading out again. At Crowell and Alcott's store on Clark Avenue and Railroad Street people could buy everything from a thimble to a plow, including dry goods, thick hams, dry salt pork, lard, bacon or kegs of beer. The clerks kept busy from early morning until late at night, when they bolted the doors and accounted for a day's business.

Coaches attached to construction and freight trains arrived crowded with prospectors on their way to the mineral fields. Hundreds continually came and left from this drunken town of tents and shacks, which behaved and resembled a typical western frontier community of Frederick Jackson Turner's classic historical interpretation.

The magic of Las Vegas lured former college professors, retired army officers, lawyers, doctors, judges, businessmen, laborers — in fact, people from most segments of society. Only slight social distinctions existed. Some had fled from trouble at home while others were wanted for various crimes in distant localities.

No one asked a newcomer where he had come from and why, or even for his full name. If he called himself "Bill" then with that name he was greeted, and further questions were unwelcome. When a stranger finally talked about himself, it was usually after he had a few drinks. Conversation then flowed freely, and in that way people finally learned about one another.

As many as 150 people camped in scattered tents and in huts along Las Vegas creek early in 1905 waiting in the wind and cold for Clark's Las Vegas townsite to open for settlement in May.

Late in April 1905 Las Vegas had about 1500 people who lived in the McWilliams townsite or along Las Vegas Creek in pitched tents, according to the Los Angeles *Times*. The rival *Examiner* was critical of the fledgling town on the desert. One reporter wrote of "freighters from the Muddy River, prospectors and miners from Crescent, gentlemen from Los Angeles and tin-horns from everywhere elbowing each other through the long streets of the tent town, taking in the sights and listening to the spieling of the shouters and the tuneless banging of the town's only piano."

This reporter also told of Las Vegans serving free flowing beer that had boiled in the sun for a day "or perhaps for a week." (All Las Vegas beer was kept on ice in bottles.) A story about two beer-drinking donkeys gave Angelenos an impression that Las Vegas had low morality standards and that there was a scarcity of legitimate industrial and social news.

Even the new Clark townsite did not escape the reporter's imagination: "Around the sacred town-site's limits is stretched a live-wire barbed fence, backed up by a dozen or fifteen husky Nevada deputy sheriffs, armed with pick handles and old style forty-fives."

By early May the McWilliams townsite was in a race for supremacy and the investors' dollars with Clark's railroad townsite. Each contracted huge quarter and half-page advertisements in the big California dailies. In one of them the McWilliams Las Vegas Townsite Company proudly boasted that its town already had a bank, six general stores, three drug stores, two wholesale houses, three furniture stores, two assay offices, many good restaurants, fourteen lodging houses, a hotel, two warehouses storing hay, grain and feed, a bottling works and two blacksmith shops. "It is sure to be a city of more than 10,000 in a short time. Come and see us..."

In comparison, nothing had been built on the Clark townsite, though immediately adjoining it on the west were a few company owned businesses. The land had been leveled by a heavy railroad

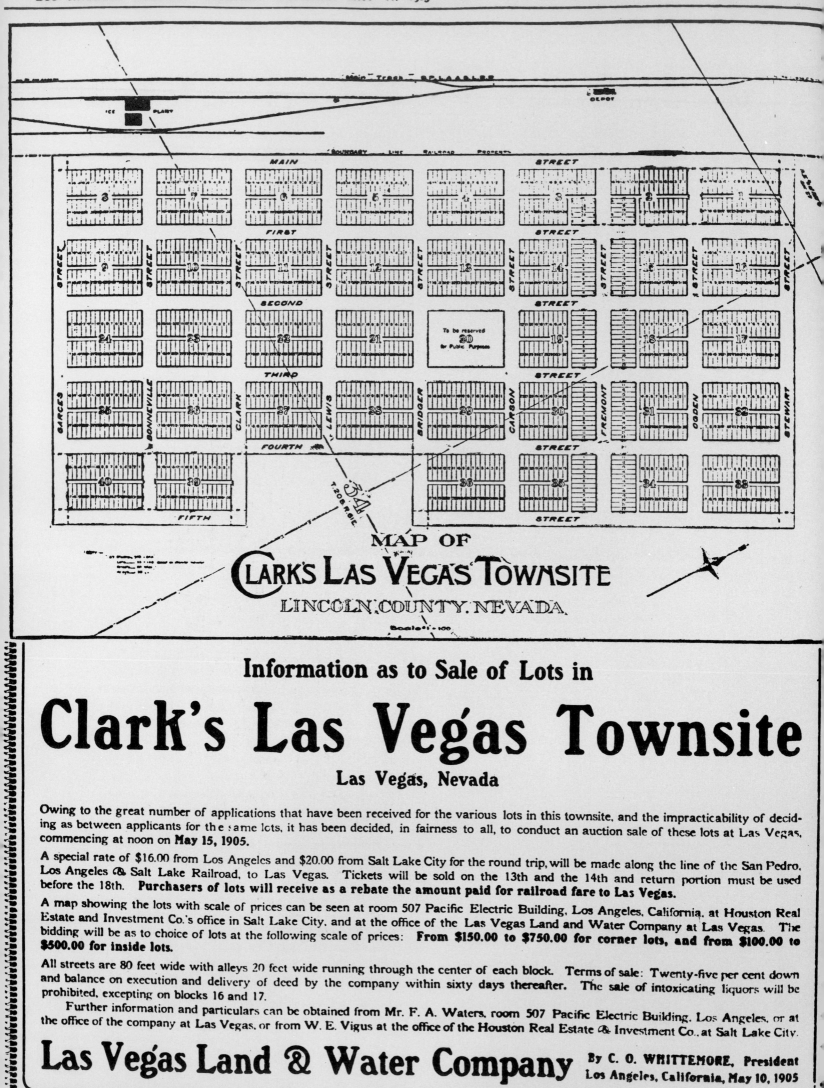

MAP OF
CLARK'S LAS VEGAS TOWNSITE
LINCOLN COUNTY, NEVADA.

Information as to Sale of Lots in

Clark's Las Vegas Townsite

Las Vegas, Nevada

Owing to the great number of applications that have been received for the various lots in this townsite, and the impracticability of deciding as between applicants for the same lots, it has been decided, in fairness to all, to conduct an auction sale of these lots at Las Vegas, commencing at noon on **May 15, 1905.**

A special rate of $16.00 from Los Angeles and $20.00 from Salt Lake City for the round trip, will be made along the line of the San Pedro, Los Angeles & Salt Lake Railroad, to Las Vegas. Tickets will be sold on the 13th and the 14th and return portion must be used before the 18th. **Purchasers of lots will receive as a rebate the amount paid for railroad fare to Las Vegas.**

A map showing the lots with scale of prices can be seen at room 507 Pacific Electric Building, Los Angeles, California, at Houston Real Estate and Investment Co.'s office in Salt Lake City, and at the office of the Las Vegas Land and Water Company at Las Vegas. The bidding will be as to choice of lots at the following scale of prices: **From $150.00 to $750.00 for corner lots, and from $100.00 to $500.00 for inside lots.**

All streets are 80 feet wide with alleys 20 feet wide running through the center of each block. Terms of sale: Twenty-five per cent down and balance on execution and delivery of deed by the company within sixty days thereafter. The sale of intoxicating liquors will be prohibited, excepting on blocks 16 and 17.

Further information and particulars can be obtained from Mr. F. A. Waters, room 507 Pacific Electric Building, Los Angeles, or at the office of the company at Las Vegas, or from W. E. Vigus at the office of the Houston Real Estate & Investment Co., at Salt Lake City.

Las Vegas Land & Water Company

By C. O. WHITTEMORE, President
Los Angeles, California, May 10, 1905.

iron weight ninety pounds to the foot, hitched to an eight horse team. The iron uprooted most of the Indian cabbage, sage, wildflowers and stubborn evergreen growth, though a gang of workers had to dig up mesquite and small trees. Stakes were driven to designate streets and lot sites.

Next to Clark's townsite, near the present Main and Stewart Streets, the Las Vegas Trading Company was hastily building the Hotel Las Vegas to accommodate land purchasers at the big sale soon to be held. That tent hostelry would have thirty rooms partitioned by canvas, as well as a lobby, a modern kitchen and dining room staffed by several experienced waitresses from the popular Hollenbeck Hotel in Los Angeles. Each room's furnishings would include iron and copper bedsteads, and a commode with a washbowl and a pitcher. The proprietors hoped that everything would be ready by Monday, May 8, the scheduled day of the land sale.

The previous day several hundred people, including saloon-keepers, gamblers, real estate investors and speculators, hard-rock miners, as well as those who did their mining in banks, all wondered whether or not the lots on which they had placed money would be theirs. But disappointment overshadowed the fervid expectation and excitement when railroad officials announced that the sale would be postponed another week because they were not ready.

On May 8 a traveling Los Angeles *Times* reporter noted about 500 visitors waiting for the land to be thrown open. He feared that rapacious speculators might create an artificial boom. The same dispatch said that nobody could adequately handle the heavy freight runs into Las Vegas because not even as much as a shed protected incoming cargo. A freight depot was needed, and construction began soon thereafter.

During the same week railroad engineers, draftsmen and clerks worked overtime to prepare for the big opening on May 15. Townsite maps posted at railroad offices from Salt Lake City to Los Angeles notified people all along the line. Lot prices were marked on the map.

Five days before the sale more than 3000 land applications already had been filed with the Los Angeles claim agent, many of which came through John S. Park in Las Vegas. For every parcel available three purchasers stood ready with money. About half of these were from Los Angeles, although some Easterners investigated the townsite and continued their journey into Los Angeles to buy directly at the railroad company offices.

Then on May 12 the railroad announced that since applications far exceeded the lots available, there would be an auction. Contracts and registrations were thus cancelled and refunds made. How this came about at such a late date involved a power struggle between the Salt Lake Railroad and the parent Union Pacific, which owned 51% of the stock, acquired after the "right of way" war east of Culverwell Ranch four years earlier.

A day or two previously W.H. Bancroft, who managed the U.P.'s interest in the S.P., L.A. & S.L., wired Clark that he preferred to sell Las Vegas lots at auction, thus giving everyone an equal chance.

Clark swiftly replied that it was impossible to do that because applications and deposits had been received for most lots.

Over the wires then came this terse message: "Auction or nothing. Bancroft."

The clamoring crowd accepted the change with enthusiasm. Action was what they wanted and the right to enter the magic boundaries, regardless of the method. In the words of one observer: "The auction was a nice clever scheme—the simplest way of giving everybody a fair shake (down)." Even the Las Vegas *Age*, though not wanting to create bad feeling against the townsite managers, believed that the railroad's methods showed little consideration for its prospective patrons.

On the evening of May 13 about 200 eager investors left Los Angeles on the Salt Lake train for the big sale. All had taken advantage of a special $16 round trip excursion fare to look over the townsite, and purchasers were guaranteed refund of their ticket. "Make your sleeper reservations early," admonished Los Angeles newspaper advertisements. A large consignment of eatables also was sent, as well as a force of waitresses for temporary service at a new cafe.

The tent Las Vegas Hotel, under construction during early May, was ready for guests the day before the auction. Fortunately, it possessed a large refrigerator full of bottled beer and a kitchen well stocked with groceries, including fresh beef slaughtered at Las Vegas Ranch. All thirty rooms soon overflowed with guests. Its cigar case was probably the best patronized one in the state.

Monday May 15 finally came. The early morning sun bounced over the mountains and met a clear blue sky. As yet no hot weather had come that year.

Around a large wooden platform under a spreading mesquite tree just north of the modern Union Plaza Hotel, more than a thousand eager land purchasers huddled to hear six foot six-inch C.O. Whittemore, president of the Las Vegas Land & Water Company, explain guarantees of future development written in each bill of sale. The railroad subsidiary would install a modern system to bring water pressure to every lot, grade and oil all streets, and build a depot and railroad shops employing hundreds of men.

Just before 10 a.m. Whittemore introduced noted Los Angeles auctioneer Ben E. Rhoades, who banged a gavel to open the sale. His ready wit, quick ear and eye and decisive fairness kept sales going at a brisk pace. Bidding had snap and vim; it was intense and determined. Many cool-headed businessmen in the good natured crowd contested for choice business locations. Three lots at the northeast corner of Main and Fremont Streets (where the present Sal Sagev Hotel is) went for $1750! An equal amount was paid for land on the opposite side of Fremont Street. Lots between Main and First Streets and fronting on Fremont sold for $850, $750 and $800!

By late morning the heat rose, yet the auctioneer kept the land-hungry mob in good humor. In the 106° heat collars wilted, and those inappropriately dressed in wool suits and dresses sought refuge in shade, with very little of it in sight. By noon it grew really warm, and so the auctioneer stopped the bidding for a two-hour lunch break. Some wandered to the Hotel Las Vegas for a cold bottle of beer and lunch.

But when the hotel proprietor threw open the front door, a hot blast hit him. An interior thermometer registered 128°! He retrieved the cold beer from the ice box and served it outside. The disappointed proprietor had failed to install a "fly" —another canvas—above the hotel roof to keep the sun's direct rays from striking the tent itself.

Additional sales were made after the auction resumed in midafternoon, but because of the heat Rhoades quit early, about 3 p.m. Of the 1200 townsite lots, 176 had been purchased for $79,566. Los Angeles money was affluent. Some had bid up to $1200 above scheduled prices for choice locations.

Las Vegas had made the map as a town. Early that evening drays and skids pulling tent and wooden houses, stores, and lodging houses, raised dust clouds that hovered above the townsite. Other great pillars rose every time a vehicle disturbed the six-inch to one-foot deep dust pockets which

Las Vegas Springs

Water Ollas

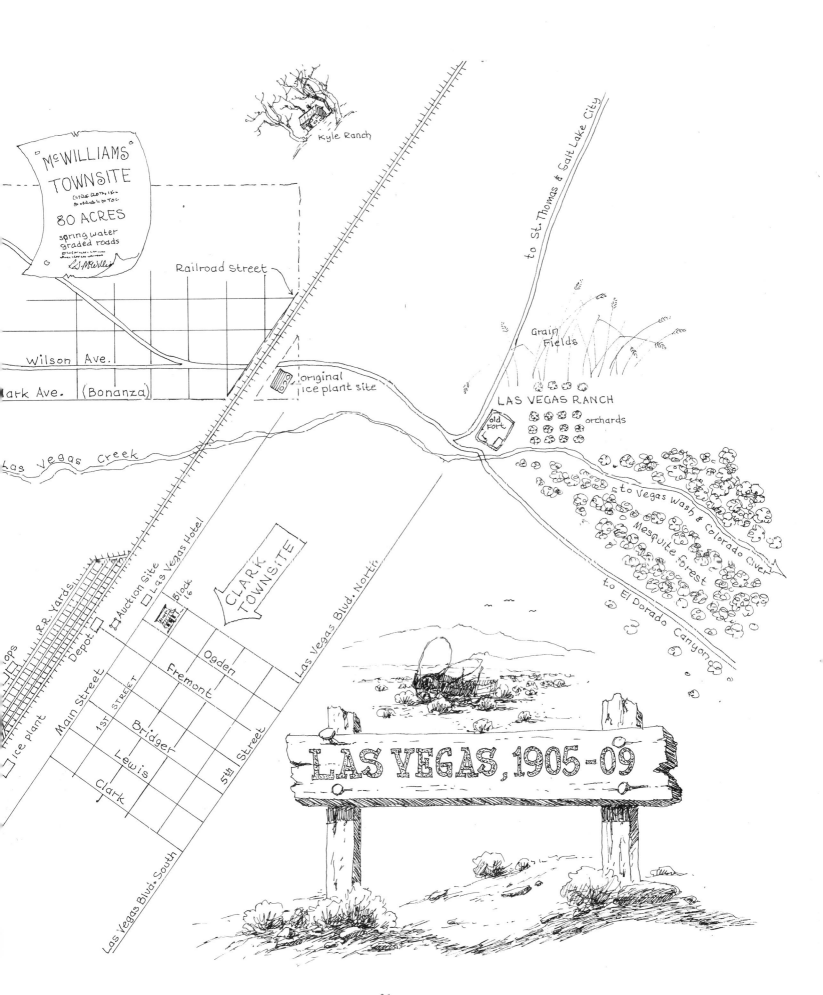

Kyle Ranch

McWILLIAMS TOWNSITE

80 ACRES

spring water
graded roads

Railroad Street

to St. Thomas & Salt Lake City

Wilson Ave.

Grain Fields

ark Ave. (Bonanza)

original ice plant site

LAS VEGAS RANCH

old Fort

orchards

Las Vegas Creek

to Vegas Wash & Colorado River

Mesquite forest

to El Dorado Canyon

R.R. Yards

Auction Site

Las Vegas Hotel

Block 16

CLARK TOWNSITE

Depot

Ogden

Las Vegas Blvd. North

ice plant

Main Street

1st Street

Fremont

Bridger

5th Street

Lewis

Clark

Las Vegas Blvd. South

LAS VEGAS, 1905-09

In the midst of Las Vegas Valley, ninety miles long by thirty wide, the San Pedro, Los Angeles & Salt Lake Railroad platted Las Vegas townsite. It had a gentle slope southeast in the direction of the Colorado River. In the picture below, railroad attorney C. O. Whittemore stands at left with pen in hand; to his left are auctioneer Rhodes and a clerk. The auction disregarded applications made at company invitation. In spirited bidding the best sites brought nearly four times the original scheduled prices. About three quarters of the lots were sold in two days, and even the lumber in the auctioneer's stand brought $7.

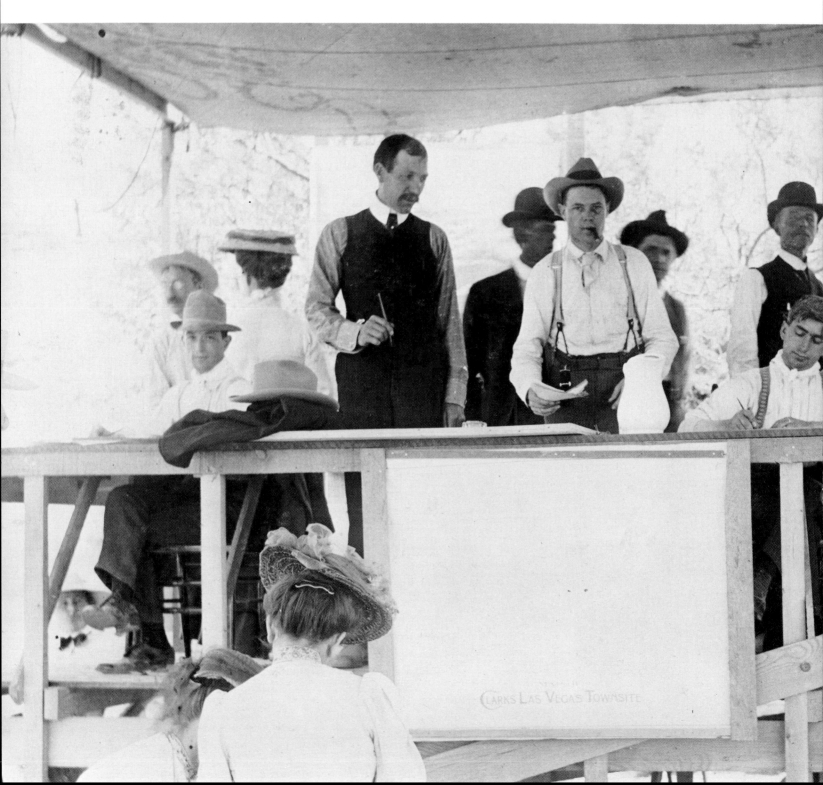

filled the street's wagon ruts. New land owners made a careful search for lot stakes among weeds and scrub bushes. Until late at night hammers and saws marked the progress of each building. A few merchants on Fremont Street and saloon men in block 16 of the townsite quickly readied their structures for business the next morning.

All day Tuesday May 16 from 8 a.m. lot sales continued, though at scheduled prices. During the two days the railroad netted about $265,000. Purchasers believed the railroad company's promises. Less desirable business and residential lots which remained unsold were placed on sale at Los Angeles and Salt Lake City.

On the Clark townsite's first Thursday night a shooting occurred at a wide open dance held in one of the newly erected saloons. Other than bedlam no serious consequences occurred. A man named "Indian Kid" was the central figure in the affray which took place somewhere along block 16. That area of town on Second Street between Ogden and Stewart Streets quickly developed into a "red-light" district.

All other property including that on Fremont Street had a "no liquor" clause in the deeds. Many would-be purchasers objected, believing that a desert town such as Las Vegas should have its liquor early, often and in abundance.

The legal liquor sales on block 16 made that property highly desirable. Hotels, restaurants and wholesale distributors could sell liquor outside of that special area. The penalty for violating the "no-liquor" clause would be title reversion to the Las Vegas Land & Water Company.

In the following months anyone wanting to open a saloon outside of block 16 provided a few rentals and called his establishment a "hotel." In mid-August 1905 the railroad's subsidiary instituted its first suit against a man for alleged violation of the "no liquor" clause. The trial proved nothing. No title was reverted, yet a cloud remained over every lot in Clark's townsite because of the controversial clause. Decades later, after World War II, the railroad rescinded the "no liquor" clause by filing a declaration with the county recorder.

Another earlier matter resolved itself soon after the auction. All during May J.T. McWilliams patiently waited while the railroad company continued building its ice plant on his triangular plot, east of the tracks and north of the Clark townsite. About two weeks after the auction McWilliams called the railroad company into account by meeting with its officials in Los Angeles and showing them that they had been building on his land. He then asked $5000 for the property.

The railroad officials were furious, both at their blundering surveyors and at McWilliams because he had not notified the railroad of its mistake earlier. Work on the ice plant stopped immediately after about $10,000 had been spent in improvements. But McWilliams waited in vain for his check, and the railroad began digging at a new site about three quarters of a mile south of McWilliams' property.

Though Clark's townsite auction had signalled the decline of the original Las Vegas, loss of the emerging ice facility also made the older town lose

In April 1905 the Las Vegas Bank and Trust Company, (bottom, opposite page) the Valley's pioneer bank, opened its office in the McWilliams' townsite, but it quickly moved to the Clark townsite after the May 15 auction. The bank folded later that same summer with no loss to depositors.

Las Vegas' second bank, (top, opposite page) managed by John S. Park, maintained temporary quarters in May 1905 in Kuhn's mercantile store, a veritable emporium opposite the depot. Sandwiches and drinks also were sold. The building to the left is an early post office.

Center of social activity in 1905 was Hotel Las Vegas, (below) a 40 x 140 canvas hostelry furnished and fitted in first class for desert accommodations. Charles "Pop" Squires, later editor of the Las Vegas Age, was the proprietor. This ungainly tent was located on the west side of North Main Street, near Stewart Avenue, adjoining the townsite on the north. The canvas and lumber for the hotel were cut to size in Los Angeles, ready to be nailed together in Las Vegas upon arrival.

Adjacent to Hotel Las Vegas was the kitchen and dining room, shown at right. Early in March 1906 these canvas buildings were torn down when the railroad company ordered all tents on its ground removed.

Block and Botkin's store on Fremont Street between First and Second Streets was the first large men's shop on the bleak Las Vegas townsite in the summer of 1905. The two-story building to its right is the Palace Hotel; the nearby tent belonged to Dr. Roy W. Martin, the town's only physician. Later the Palace became the hospital.

At middle is the town's pioneer bakery. When most businesses folded their tents and moved from the McWilliams townsite to the Clark townsite, Vegas Home Bakery's bake ovens were too heavy and hot to move. An early journalist commented, "By using Vegas Home Bakery's bread many couples are today living joyfully together who might have been divorced had they continued using home made thuds and cement biscuits."

Sleek stages regulary traveled through the desert between Las Vegas and Bullfrog in 1905. They were the last word in transportation.

prominence. For several weeks after the auction the movement of business and residents to the railroad townsite continued. The Imperial Hotel was torn down, loaded in a wagon and re-erected. The Las Vegas *Age's* fireproof building was put on rollers at its Wilson Avenue location and set in place on a new site on Second Street within three days time. By the beginning of summer the original townsite (also called "Ragtown") looked pathetically unkempt. Small fires had destroyed several tents and shacks, including the town's theatre.

Yet the old town was not completely hopeless. Some businessmen at Ragtown continued to maintain profitable hotels, cafes, stores and stables to accommodate the transient crowd. After a hard run from the Bullfrog, swampers and skinners equipped their wagons there and stage drivers discharged their passengers.

What a strange sight it was to see the Bullfrog stage arrive! For almost sixty hours the passengers had been on the road. Cramped and stiff from the long non-stop ride, they stepped down from the stage like animated clay statues. But the very dirt which covered them was said to be laden with gold dust. They had breathed the germs at Bullfrog and had caught the gold fever. How contagious it was! In an instant the madness over minerals spread to the surrounding crowd, and thereafter followed delirious talk of fractions, dips, spurs, angles and ore shipments from Goldfield, and stocks, leads, options and assays from Bullfrog. Rumors spread from saloon to hotel, and the word soon went throughout the nation.

The fantastic amount of freight and stage traffic which churned the thoroughfares of both Las Vegas townsites would stagger the modern mind. Especially around sunrise, but continuing throughout the day and night, a steady procession of eight- to twenty-animal teams drawing high-wheeled freight wagons each loaded with immense quantities of supplies and equipment, whiskey, animal feed, machinery, and more whiskey, struck out for Bullfrog and adjacent camps, or returned with empty wagons and one or two trailers for another cargo.

Early in June 1905 nearly 1500 horses hauled freight wagons from Las Vegas to the Bullfrog mining district. The Porter Brothers employed 120 horses; another Rhyolite firm had 105. As many as fifty freighters daily passed each other on the Las Vegas-Bullfrog run. The corrals in Las Vegas were filled nearly every night with coaches and freighting outfits.

Also in Las Vegas from early morning until dark, local teams ploughed through the streets to and fro in every direction, conveying lumber and other materials to sustain the marvelous building boom. Close upon their heels from the freight depot came countless other rigs, each with drayloads of merchandise for the new businesses that every setting sun saw completed. These private outfits mingled with burros that often began braying early in the morning. Their loud hee-haws violated both tune and tone.

These "Nevada mockingbirds" often ran up and down the streets scavenging trash barrels. They liked colored paper especially on bright tin cans, probably licking them for the glue. A stray burro which spotted exposed rubbish often stood beside it and brayed as if calling others by the hee-hawing. Water supplies had to be carefully guarded. An early Las Vegan had to chase away burros from his tent because they would scratch themselves on the poles and topple it over.

The many mules, horses and burros attracted countless flies which swarmed around the feed yards and through the town. Only a few tents and shacks had screens and even then flies managed to crawl through crevices. Behind the drapery of dust and sweat the airy canvas mansions in month-old Las Vegas housed not only bachelors but also the wives and daughters of fortune-seeking husbands and fathers.

A typical tent home consisted of canvas stretched over a lumber frame built on top of a wooden box with three foot walls. Some possessed a wooden floor, while others had mere adobe dirt. If sprinkled often the latter formed a good hard surface, though dampness made it unpleasant to walk on. Home-made rugs or old burlap often covered bare floors.

Women pasted or pinned to the walls pictures and photos of pleasant memories at other homes. A double cot covered by a bright colored quilt with matching pillows served as a bed. The only table was used first to prepare meals and then to serve them. Afterwards, it became a reading, writing or sewing table.

One corner contained a stove and a cupboard made of cracker boxes. A few chairs completed the furniture. A solitary trunk held everything that would be inside the closet of a dozen bureau drawers and chiffonier in a city bedroom. There were no unnecessary household articles for social use; nothing was kept in a tent home that was not used every day. Though a canvas abode looked

Few women made homes on the desert by choice. Most of them followed her man to Las Vegas while he sought wealth here. For a woman the elusive secret of happy tent life was to have a clean house.

Las Vegas Ranch is the setting for these three pictures. In the bath house (above) water diverted from Las Vegas Creek ran through the sawed board in the foreground and into a wooden tub sunk in the ground. A plank is provided to step on while drying off, and thick matting covers the bare earth. Canvas curtains provided privacy. The bed in the tent is made with the quilt neatly tucked.

In the top picture on the opposite page, the housekeeper is beside her tent near the corral area. At bottom is a boy cutting lumber with a bucksaw; it had a flexible cutting edge with a turnbuckle tension blade to keep the saw straight. The costly lumber shipped in is used inadvisably to make pathways across muddy areas. To protect the living area from the sun's fiery rays, a wooden "fly" was built above each tent. Tents without these covers usually had sides that rolled up to provide ventilation.

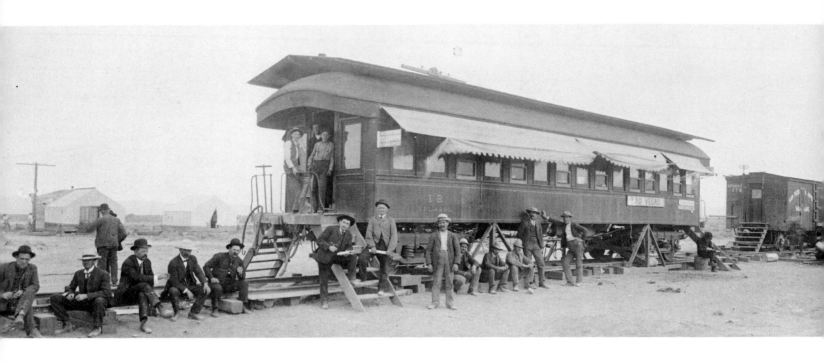

In 1905 a railroad coach (left) housed the Las Vegas depot and ticket office, as well as desks for Western Union Telegraph and Pacific Fruit Express Company. At center, the freight depot is shown as it looked around June 1905. Later that same summer a more permanent building replaced these primitive facilities. The principal method of travel to Las Vegas was by train, and one of the first ones through is shown at bottom.

crude, an imaginative woman could maintain a comfortable home in Las Vegas.

For protection against the sun, tent houses had above them a canvas "fly" or a board roof. The largest tents also had a porch both in front and rear, carpeted floors or prairie grass rugs, willow furniture, and walls decorated with art squares and burlap or Japanese matting. Curtains usually divided tents into rooms.

Gas lanterns provided light, water was stored in barrels adjacent to the tent, and perishables maintained their freshness in a crude desert cooler. The latter consisted of a wooden box tightly wrapped in burlap or blankets. One end of the material extended upward into a small metal container kept filled with water. As the water steadily seeped through the material around the box, evaporation kept its contents cool. Water dripping from a kerosene can onto a burlap-wrapped box produced the same result.

Tent houses were easily portable. Even the largest dwelling could be placed on a wagon and moved without much disturbance. In June 1905 most Las Vegans lived in tents because of a scarcity of building materials, as the railroad could not ship in lumber fast enough to meet the demand. Local dealers incurred a full share of abuse because of the wood famine.

Lack of materials affected the local labor market. Around June 1 carpenters were paid $4.00 a day, while laborers received from $2.00 to $2.50 a day. Yet other merchandise seemed to be in abundance. During that same week one observer counted eighty carloads of materials in the railroad yards.

A justice of the peace maintained the dignity of the new town, though little disorder had occurred that spring. People generally minded their own business, following the unwritten law of most frontier towns. But an unmarked grave told of the sudden death of one man caught stealing animal feed. This and similar incidents made a Goodsprings merchant admonish a friend going to Las Vegas: "Now put this gun in your belt and be careful. That's a tough town over there and they tell me they get a man for breakfast pretty near every morning."

Railroad ties placed on end made the first jail, though an old steel cage of strap metal and tin had to be placed inside the wooden cell to minimize the danger of fire. The bed consisted of two metal frames fastened against the wall. Late in May two women were kept there for allegedly inducing a wealthy New Yorker to drink a glass of "Mumm's" in which knockout drops had been spilled. The morning after, the victim awoke on the desert robbed of about $1000 and his gold watch.

As summer approached, the jail became too hot for occupancy. Some prisoners were hauled to Las Vegas Creek, where around large cottonwood trees growing about fifteen feet from the water heavy log chains had been placed. Fastened to them were smaller chains which connected to the prisoner's ankle or wrists. The long chain allowed the prisoner to drink water from the creek and follow the shade of the cottonwood trees during the day. Twice daily the prisoners were handcuffed and led away to eat.

The burgeoning town derived some revenue by taxing businesses. Hotels paid $8.50 per quarter; restaurants, livery stables and boarding houses paid the same rate. Real estate agents were charged $21 per quarter. One certain undertaker, who had done no business, nevertheless paid $12. He also opened a furniture store and was assessed an additional similar amount. Peddlers paid $11 per month but if they used a horse the rate was $26. The town charged gambling establishments $76 per month—in advance! Late in May, doctors and lawyers had yet to be assessed. A tamale man paid $11 per month to keep the people warm at night.

Prices of goods varied. Beer averaged fifty cents a bottle, and late in May more than a hundred barrels were sold daily. Meals started at fifteen cents. Beds cost two bits to a dollar a night. The town's only bath house had but one tub; a person wanting to bathe or cool himself paid a quarter and remained in the water until called out. On hot days the tub was occupied at all hours. Nights were chilly, however, and a blanket was needed for comfort.

In addition to the heat, windstorms and sandstorms brought added discomfort and destruction. About June 1 strong winds bent and twisted several buildings under construction, blowing down one frame structure and wrestling with tattered tents. Tumbleweeds wheeled like drunken acrobats through the townsite.

Another destroyer, fire, first visited Las Vegas on June 6. Because of it, the new town made front page news for the first time in the Los Angeles press. The blaze started in the kitchen of "Chop House Bill's" on North First Street, when a helper tried to fill the tank of a lighted stove. In less than five minutes leaping flames embraced adjacent structures. Vocal alarm and the shrill whistle of a

Poker chips are piled almost chin high during a game in one of the local tent and wooden saloons. A mirror and pictures of women (including one on the far wall holding a pail of beer) adorn the wall, and at the hastily constructed wooden bar a burro is begging for beer.

Las Vegas first brick building contained a drug store and the store of Crowell & Alcott, pioneer valley merchants. When this building was completed in July 1905 on North Main Street, potted plants were placed in front of it. Note the heavily laden burro.

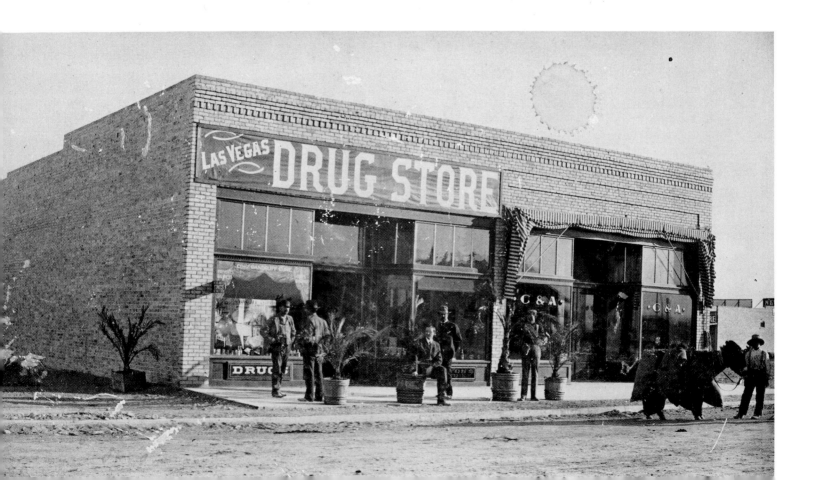

Los Vegas post office first opened on Las Vegas Ranch in December 1893, but almost a decade later the spelling was changed to the present name. Early in 1905 the office moved to the McWilliams townsite, which is possibly the top view, but by June it was relocated adjacent to the Kuhn mercantile store, shown on page 84. Another early building probably on the same site, is shown at right. On Sundays, it was open until midnight. About that time a citizen's group initiated a proposal to rename the town simply "Vegas" to avoid confusion with the older New Mexico town with the same name. By 1907 letters were picked up in more spacious quarters (below) on Fremont in the First State Bank building, where boxes were installed for the first time.

railroad switch engine summoned several dozen men to the scene, but with no water or chemicals nothing could be done except rescue some furnishings.

In all the blaze consumed four buildings. By aid of a bucket brigade and wet blankets, an adjoining bank was protected from danger. Losses were complete because no insurance company would take risks in Las Vegas. Eleven days later, when a spark from a passing locomotive ignited oil on the tracks and spread fire to nearby coal chutes, concerned Las Vegans took steps toward organizing a volunteer fire department.

By the time Las Vegas was a month old its people in a wild building crusade had erected nearly every kind of establishment. Though several sturdy frame buildings had been finished, tents still contained saloons, the post office, hotels and a bank. Organized religion had not yet come to Las Vegas. Churches had to wait their turn for the energy, money and interest of the new residents. The staccato sound of hammers and the rasping of saws continued around the clock and permanent houses magically sprang up.

When a saloon man began building his establishment he first installed the bar. Then while construction continued on the sides and the roof, business went merrily on. Rapping hammers harmonized with the clinking of glasses, and though saw-

dust spilled into the beer and nails dropped on the lunch no one objected because it was all taken in stride.

In this land of sweat and toil, bums infested the town with the mistaken idea that gold lay on the desert and in the streets, free for the taking. Rapacious real estate men invested heavily in hopes of quick sales and big profits. A few squatters took up land near a stone covered area and sold wagonloads of gravel to local contractors. One small-time schemer with a $50 bill ate at a certain restaurant. Since the manager could not change it, he told the customer to call again. Before leaving town, he had worked nearly every Las Vegas cafe.

Many Nevada newspapers were optimistic about the success of the new town. An editor at Rhyolite thought that Las Vegas, "the creature of a day, so to speak," would soon exceed in size any Nevada town except Reno, Tonopah and Goldfield. But a Kingman, Arizona resident who came to look for business possibilities believed that Las Vegas would soon settle down to be a placid railroad town such as Needles, California, because there was nothing to justify continuing the boom.

A recession set in at Las Vegas during the next month, July. It had overbuilt and some businessmen lost heart. Not less than 26 Las Vegas business licenses were returned to the county during the next several weeks. Freight shipments through

Salt Lake railroad photographers Ramsey and Pierce took this picture just after sunrise one spring day in 1905, when these two supply-laden rigs were ready to head out of Las Vegas for Beatty and Bullfrog. Captain Gibson (seated on the far right) drove one of the long-line outfits for the Rose and Palmer store at Beatty after the regular driver had become drunk a few miles out of town and could

not manage the team. Since he got abusive by shouting obscenities and theatening to kill anyone in sight, Gibson lassoed him and tied him up before turning him over to a stage driver returning to Las Vegas. Gibson battled poor roads, the heat, dust and wind to complete the delivery through the deserts enroute to Beatty.

Las Vegas also declined because of poor road conditions between Las Vegas and Bullfrog. Private delivery autos incurred the wrath of animal drawn freighters because the latter believed that autos tore up the road. Much of the Bullfrog trade began to be shipped by railroad to Goldfield and Ivanpah, California. From those points freighters completed the haul. The Ivanpah-Bullfrog run was blessed with plenty of water and feed, especially at the Manse Ranch in Pahrump Valley.

One of the teamsters, Captain Ray Gibson, continued to use the Las Vegas-Bullfrog road. It took only a day to load his big wagons and trailers with supplies and animal feed, but additional time was needed if horses had to be shod or wagons repaired at the blacksmith shop. Las Vegas had better facilities than Beatty. The last thing Gibson did was fill the water barrels and water and feed the animals.

The first day ended at Tule Springs, where it was possible to stop next to springs to obtain water

to fill barrels that had been tapped or leaking. At Indian Springs, the second night stop, a pool held many small trout. Eating and overnight accommodations for stage travelers were available. The third night was a dry camp between Indian Springs and Ash Meadows, reached on the fourth night. That was a welcome spa in the middle of sandy deserts. The remaining forty miles to Beatty took two or maybe three days, with dry camps made each night.

But in that very summer, 1905, the days of animal teams were numbered after a private group announced late in June that it would begin using four large desert-adapted, 115 horsepower autos on the Las Vegas-Bullfrog run. Thereafter motor car and horse team dueled to the death, though each operated with disadvantages. Auto drivers often encountered an overheated engine, wheels which sank in sand as high as the hubs, and lengthy delays because of a lack of repair facilities. Extra gas and tires and other spare parts had to be carried. But mechanical transport could haul two tons of goods in less than two days at most, in comparison with small freight teams which could haul six or seven tons of supplies in as many days. Larger 16 or 18 animal teams could carry up to 18 tons of mixed freight, though they also had to carry large amounts of hay and water.

On June 9 the Salt Lake Railroad announced that it would begin an auto passenger line to Bullfrog from Las Vegas, where direct train connections would be made. Thus Rhyolite would be within a days travel of Los Angeles by train and auto stage. This new service was instituted while railroad crews under Francis M. "Borax" Smith began preparing a grade out of Las Vegas in the direction of Bullfrog.

Meats, fruits and provisions in cold storage would in time be hauled in desert-equipped autos to Bullfrog, as soon as the big $100,000 Armour & Company ice and cold storage plant under construction at Las Vegas would be completed. A Rhyolite restaurant then could phone Armour one night and expect delivery by the next evening. This became a reality late in August when the ice plant began manufacturing forty to fifty tons of ice daily.

That same month a railroad subsidiary, the Nevada Rapid Transit Company, completed a private $50,000 auto road from Las Vegas to Indian Springs. There passengers disembarked for the night and caught the Bullfrog stage the next morning. In the summer heat a gang of brush pullers using a "go-devil" (a railroad iron employed as a harrow), scrapers and plows, as well as gravelmen

and shovelmen began grading and improving the road north of Indian Springs. Freight trucks averaged eleven miles an hour over the road's new coarse gravel surface.

The auto stage and animal freighter would soon be replaced by the iron horse. Initially, "Borax" Smith began building his Tonopah & Tidewater Railroad north from Las Vegas toward Death Valley and Bullfrog, but in August 1905 all work stopped after the sub-grade had been completed only about nine miles to a point near Tule Springs. Smith and Clark disagreed over rates of freight delivered by the Salt Lake railroad. Ultimately Smith built the Tonopah & Tidewater Railroad from Ludlow, California past Death Valley and into Beatty, commencing through service late in 1907.

Beginning about the first day of summer 1905 the Las Vegas Land & Water Company fulfilled its promises to lot purchasers by grading, rolling and graveling seven miles of city streets, installing cement curbs in the business district and redwood curbs in the residential areas, and laying pipes to bring water to every lot. Mains six to eight inches wide were placed underground, and hydrants were on many corners. In all, the improvements cost about $50,000. Sidewalks were not installed and people walked in the middle of streets before autos took over. With plenty of water available at a flat rate per lot, residents planted extra large lawns and set their fences near the curb.

Las Vegas' first school term was held that summer in a tent under the cottonwoods near Las Vegas Creek. One young woman taught a few dozen children, but during the first fall term more than 200 students crowded into a new wood-frame building on the corner of Second and Lewis Streets.

After the summer business slump Las Vegas experienced a building boom involving construction of solid business blocks. Meanwhile, the original Las Vegas townsite met with disaster. On the evening of September 5, bells rang as dark rolling smoke ascended skyward. "Old town is burning up!" was the cry. Many from the railroad townsite rushed there, but the fierce blaze had already done its work. Railroad Street, that once busy commercial boulevard, was reduced to ashes.

The editor of the Las Vegas *Times* lamented: "The old town is but a memory...in its day it was a roisterer with all the vitality and spirit of a typical frontier rag town. Bustle, hustle and jostle was its lot in its heyday. All this is gone. Fire has consumed it...no hope remains, like the Phoenix of old, that the town would rise again."

Thereafter, riotous block 16 was the only seat of pleasure. Nearly every night, including Christmas, it ran full blast. The Gem, the Red Onion, the Turf, the Favorite, the Double-O, the Star, the Arcade saloons and the Arizona Club were continually crowded with sharp-eyed dealers and boosters and men standing around trying to solve the mysteries of gaming. All night long sounded the strains of music, the rattle of ivory chips and the clink of silver and gold coins on the tables of faro, roulette, craps, black jack and poker. Standing room around the stoves was at a premium in the winter.

Outside the saloons but conveniently nearby, small establishments sported prostitutes. At the dance halls these "beautiful" ladies waited to bestow their affections for a consideration. That part of Las Vegas looked like a rip-roaring, whiskey-drinking, gun-toting, gambling town, while the rest of the town was conservative and business-like.

Beginning in 1906 the Pacific Fruit Express Company provided power. Later, that company developed into the Consolidated Power & Telegraph Company, which also supplied gas. Business to the Bullfrog district increased when the

Las Vegas & Tonopah Railroad was completed to Beatty in October 1906.

In 1907, culture came to the desert town, though it almost did not. While the opera house block was being built on the corner of First and Fremont Streets, its freshly laid walls, supported by insufficient bracing, partially fell down during a severe night windstorm. The building was soon repaired, and it also served as a public meeting and lodge hall, and for a time as a "moving picture" theatre. Fire claimed it in the spring of 1912.

Las Vegans experienced hardships later in 1907 because of the nationwide financial panic. The local First State Bank remained solvent. Also in 1907 a test well sunk three miles north of town determined that Las Vegas Valley contained large bodies of artesian water. From that small beginning, well drilling soon reached large proportions. Five years later water from about a hundred wells irrigated several thousand acres of ranchland and homesites.

In the summer of 1908 campaigns by the aggressive Las Vegas Promotion Society began publicizing the town. Its initial project was to encourage the creation of a county with its seat at Las Vegas.

A railroad subsidiary installed high redwood curbs (opposite page) such as those at First and Ogden Streets in the fall of 1905. This two-room school on the southwest corner of Second and Lewis Streets had rooms finished in cloth and paper with a patch board ceiling. Earlier that same year the building was the Salt Lake Hotel, but it was easily remodeled for only $700, including the addition of a pot-bellied stove.

Along block 16 during the daytime, everyone sought refuge in the shade, but the evening coolness late in the summer of 1905 brought out the whiskey drinkers and the girls. One observer who came to Las Vegas at that time noted that saloons outnumbered all other types of business houses combined. The establishments shown here were on the east side of North First Street between Ogden and Stewart Streets. Local delivery wagons (opposite page) and four- and six-horse rigs (below) heavily laden with hay and feed mingled in Las Vegas' dusty streets.

By the fall of 1905 Las Vegas was no longer a town of tent and wooden houses. Important early Las Vegas homes are under construction above. The prominent house is the John S. Park residence, on the northeast corner of Fourth and Fremont Streets. Note the redwood curbs. To the right, across Fremont Street, are two other partly built brick houses which are shown two decades later (below) surrounded by cottonwood and umbrella trees. These are the residences of Charles "Pop" Squires and Sina Norris. The other views at right show the Park family buggy and

Mrs. William S. Park, whose husband was a dentist and son of banker Park. These fine residences were later eliminated by the spread of the Fremont Street commercial district.

FIRST TRAIN TO OFFICIALLY ENTER BULLFROG DISTRICT. BACK FOTO

Without governmental assistance and against the violent opposition of an established railroad system, the genius of Senator William A. Clark of Montana persisted during 1902-05. With the San Pedro, Los Angeles & Salt Lake Railroad he spanned the Southwest with iron rails, shortening the travel time between Los Angeles and Salt Lake City to little more than a day. With that project completed in the spring of 1905, Clark later that year started building the Las Vegas & Tonopah Railroad from a point one mile south of Las Vegas to Beatty, 114 miles north, completing the line in October of the following year. One of the first trains to use the new rails is shown above.

Clark's line was the very first to reach the allegedly rich Bullfrog mining district, but within months two railroads coming from other directions were competing for the diminishing business. Trains ran from Las Vegas to Beatty until 1918, when the line was abandoned after several years of red-ink operations. The steel rails were ripped up, shipped to the Pacific Coast, loaded on ships and used to build a railroad in China. The ties were used to build walls for many farm buildings and houses both in Beatty and Las Vegas and kept both towns in firewood for many years. The L.V. & T. timetable dates to February 1908.

Around 1905 logs were brought to the sawmill in Lee Canyon in the Spring Mountains by horse team. A driver sitting on top of the logs manned the jerkline which extended to the lead animals. The large stack provided an extra long draft for the boiler which was fueled by slabs and sawdust. A steam tractor delivered the finished timber to Owens siding on the Las Vegas & Tonopah Railroad, twelve miles east, for delivery to Goldfield, Las Vegas and Bullfrog. Because of the steepness of the return trip, a climb of about 5100 feet, the tractors cached water on the descent for use on the uphill run.

COUNTY DIVISION

Rousing Mass Meeting--Campaign Opened With Great Enthusiasm--Success Assured

As a result of action by a non-partizan committee of substantial and representative business men, a mass meeting was held Thursday evening to discuss County seat matters and determine on a plan of campaign which will remove the disadvantages suffered by the south half of Lincoln County in its transaction of County business. The great interest which our people take in this matter was shown by the large number of enthusiastic citizens present at the opera house. Many ladies were present showing the keen interest felt by them in this movement.

The Las Vegas Band enlivened the occasion with good music.

The meeting was called to order by A. W. Jurden, who after a brief outline of the work of the committee on arrangements, introduced Hon. W. R. Thomas, who acted as chairman of the meeting, and Frank A. Clark, the secretary.

After a full discussion it was plain that the sentiment in favor of County Division, instead of removal of the County seat, was overwhelming. A spirit of fairness to our neighbors of the northern portion of the county was shown by the feeling that, if the county seat should be removed to Las Vegas, they would be subjected to the same inconviences, although in a lesser degree, that we now suffer.

The meeting unanimously adopted strong resolutions favoring County Division, setting forth unanswerable arguments in its favor. A red hot campaign was favored to be carried on vigorously from now until the polls close on election day.

The Resolution adopted is now referred to as our "Declaration of Independence" and will be found on another page of this issue.

A campaign committee absolutely non-partsian in character was formed, with power to add to its number as it may see fit, composed of the following representative men.

H. M. Lillis, A. W. Jurden, F. A. Clark, Al James, W. R. Bracken, Judge Beal, W. R. Thomas, Dan Hickey, Harley Harmon, J. F. Miller, Peter Buol, W. E. Hawkins, C. W. Watson, A. N. Pauff, Chris N. Brown, W. J. Stewart, E. J. Rossell, C. P. Squires, Chas. Ireland and E. W. Griffith.

CHAPTER SIX

How Clark County
Was Created

UNTIL THE FOUNDING OF CLARK COUNTY ON JULY 1, 1909, Las Vegas was in the southern part of Lincoln, a county that covered all of southeastern Nevada. Lincoln was carved out of Nye County on February 20, 1866, when Nevada was in its infancy. Months later, after territorial acquisitions from Utah and Arizona Territories, Lincoln County attained limits which were not disturbed until the division in 1909.

Throughout the 19th century and early in this century the town of Pioche successfully governed that huge 18,576 square mile county, then the nation's second largest. County population centered at Pioche and surrounding valleys, and after 1892 at Delamar also.

Early in this century new mining booms and the building of the San Pedro, Los Angeles & Salt Lake Railroad through Lincoln County rearranged its population centers. By 1905 two distinct sections had emerged. In the north was Pioche, Delamar, and a new freighting center called Caliente. The southern end had agricultural settlements in Moapa and Virgin Valleys, mining camps at Goodsprings, Nelson and Searchlight, and the rapidly emerging railroad town of Las Vegas.

Lincoln County was fast developing into an unwieldy social and governmental unit. As early as mid-1905 the county's southern citizens discussed county division or relocation of the courthouse to Las Vegas or Searchlight.

During the weeks before Las Vegas' founding on May 15, 1905, the establishment of a bank and a newspaper—the *Age*—at a temporary Las Vegas townsite figured prominently in the Lincoln County division controversy during the next three and a half years.

That summer the Las Vegas *Age* began discussing a change because it had heard that the deteriorated courthouse in Pioche might be condemned. The editor admonished its readers: "Before the political financiers of Pioche saddle another courthouse debt on the county through the building of another courthouse, the south half should get out from under by division of the county."

The county debt, amounting to approximately $630,000 in 1905, had grown largely because of mismanagement during court-house construction, compound interest on discounted county bonds and subsequent dubious refinancing after the decline of mining at Pioche.

In 1905 Lincoln County was growing everywhere except at Pioche, and thus the cry for a shift southward of the county seat. Searchlight reportedly had about 1200 residents and a transient population of a few hundred more. Las Vegas numbered nearly as many, and Goodsprings and Nelson had a few hundred each. Searchlight was more than twice the size of the county seat.

Sectionalism beyond the talking stage initially surfaced in August 1905, when the county commissioners awarded to the *Age* all county printing and job work. The 46 year old *Lincoln County Record* at Pioche denounced the move. It likened the *Age* to a mushroom fungi of uncertain life, possessing a readership of "floaters, the shiftless and the reckless class". The *Record* encountered irregularities, such as the *Age's* failing to file a bond, and the commissioners rescinded the action.

The editor of the *Record* also had another laugh over an item in the Las Vegas paper. After commenting on a new brand of whiskey called "Sheepherder's Delight", which caused a peddler to steal his own pack and hide it in the woods, the *Record* chided the *Age* for publishing an article and crediting another newspaper for it when the *Age* had originally printed it only a short time before. "The quality of the water down at Vegas must be bad."

In November the Las Vegas *Age* ultimately won the bid for county printing because it had presented to the county commissioners specified prices for all types of jobs, while all other county papers furnished incomplete bids. In December, when Las Vegas was barely six months old, the town assumed another function which the county seat could not perform for itself. The First State Bank became the official depository of county funds, replacing a Salt Lake City bank. There was none at Pioche.

As 1905 ended the county seat removal question became quite lively and pertinent. The growing towns of Searchlight, Las Vegas and Caliente vied for the honor, while Pioche that year had little besides abandoned mines and ruined milling machinery. Its lonely streets were lined by shambles of buildings with roofs caved by the weighty snows of many winters. Some structures had not been occupied since the decline of the camp in 1892.

Southern Nevadans were at first divided between county division and courthouse removal from Pioche to Searchlight or Las Vegas. Politicians who had financial interests at stake opposed a division because one county was easier and cheaper to control than two smaller counties—it was easier to manipulate one election than two! The Salt Lake railroad preferred a shift of the county seat rather than a division because it probably feared increased taxation. The Las Vegas *Age* favored division because it thought that the north would accept that over removal of the courthouse from Pioche.

During 1906, Searchlight began publicizing a campaign for the county seat, with the local *Bulletin* leading the attack. It seemed that the number of voters in the county election of 1906 would in part determine the fate of the courthouse. The Searchlight forces frantically searched the surrounding deserts to register every possible voter. Boosters in Las Vegas combed the brush and the nearby mesquite forests for electors.

All anxiously waited for the county clerk at Pioche to announce the number of voters in Lincoln County's towns. When registration closed late in October, the largest clusters of voters were in the south: Las Vegas had 320 and Searchlight an identical number. That Las Vegas could register as many voters as the booming mining metropolis greatly encouraged the Las Vegas forces, and

Ever since its construction 1872, the courthouse at Pioche shown as it appeared the next year, has had a most scandalous financial history. Added to the original $26,400 cost were extravagant outlays such as balconies and lineoleum on the stairway. After the decline of Pioche in 1875, bonds were discounted and this coupled with dubious refinancing brought the cost of this building to Lincoln County taxpayers to approximately $800,000 by the time the courthouse debt was finally paid off in 1938.

thereafter they began to clamor for a division of the county with Las Vegas as county seat.

But only a few weeks later Pioche stirred from almost fifteen years of dormancy, reviving to the extent that a bank opened there at the end of December 1906. It would soon figure prominently in the county division skirmish. Piochers insisted that some county funds should be kept at the county seat, and demanded that county treasurer Ed Clark of Las Vegas transfer some of the money on deposit in Las Vegas. Clark refused to comply with the request, and his inaction became a central issue in the treasurer's race during the next election, November 1908.

The first seven months of 1908 were a lull before a storm of controversy that developed after July 30, to last until the November election. In a rousing mass meeting in Las Vegas at the end of July, its citizens unanimously adopted strong resolutions favoring county division, and passed a "declaration of independence" that set forth various arguments for a new county. The Lincoln County Division Club would carry out the plan, and businessmen contributed $1630 to create a work fund.

Since Lincoln County was growing both in the north and the south and could support separate county governments, Las Vegans believed that a county split would result in ease and economy for all. In addition to dealing with an unsympathetic county government, Las Vegans also faced these problems:

Immense Lincoln County was too large and unwieldy for effective administration from Pioche. Travel expenses for parties to a suit made litigation unbearable for the average southern citizen and thus only the rich could afford redressing of wrongs. With two governments thousands of dollars would be saved which otherwise would be spent in transporting witnesses, jurors, commissioners, criminals, indigents and others to Pioche on official business.

The 466-mile round trip from Searchlight to Pioche equaled the distance between New York and Boston. A courthouse at Las Vegas would be only 55 miles from Searchlight. Any south end community was at least 107 miles from the Pioche courthouse; no town in the proposed new county would be more than 100 miles from Las Vegas by ordinary conveyance.

At Pioche, the courthouse clique wondered whether or not the county bondholders would accept the obligation of the new counties for pro-

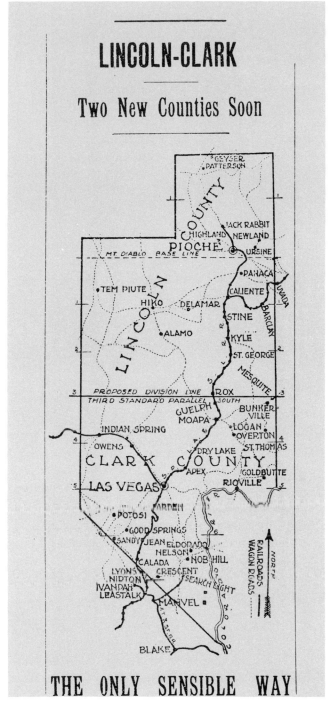

As a boost for county division, the Las Vegas Age published this map several times in 1908 and early 1909.

portional parts of the debt, adjusted to valuations. Could Lincoln County, the present debtor, legally transfer its obligation to the new counties of Clark and Lincoln?

Since the Salt Lake Railroad owned most of the county bonds, the editor of the Age brushed aside the arguments emanating from Pioche. Moreover, the railroad already had endorsed county division.

The reelection of incumbent Ed W. Clark in the 1908 Lincoln County treasurer's race meant that county funds would remain in Las Vegas. An avalanche of votes from Pioche and Searchlight sent him skidding out of office. Clark regained political prominence a year later by being appointed the first Clark County treasurer.

After a meeting on August 22, 1908, the Division Club circulated petitions to the conventions of both major political parties which met early in September, asking for their endorsement on county division. The issue dominated discussion of both conventions, and each ultimately approved of the movement.

A real fight developed in the Democratic platform committee. Searchlight's delegates stood firmly with Pioche's in opposing the division scheme, objecting to the placing of the matter in the party platform. Those two towns made strange political companions; Searchlight, though the southernmost town in the county, surprised the Las Vegas boosters by its hostility.

The Searchlight crowd opposed dividing Lincoln County because of economic reasons. Though agreeing with the fine arguments about convenience and travel costs, citizens of Searchlight disagreed with the financing of the new county. "When it comes down to dollars and cents, that is where we get off," wrote the editor of the Searchlight *Bulletin.* The paper admonished the Division Club to get out a trial balance and examine income and expenditures. "Never mind repeating about the expense to individuals—we've had that dinged into us a-plenty."

During September, petitions asking for the division circulated throughout the county. But developments in the race for County treasurer turned the election campaign into an exciting battle. The banking of county funds became the prime issue, and inextricably tied to it was the division controversy.

Incumbent Democrat Ed W. Clark was easily favored to win another two year term until late in September when another Democrat, Henry H. Lee, who lived near the county seat, became an independent candidate. Clark earlier had avowed that he would continue to maintain county funds in Las Vegas instead of transferring them to Pioche. By taking that position many believed that Clark personally wanted to dictate the appointment of the next Lincoln County treasurer, if county division were effected.

Lee became an independent candidate after northerners circulated a petition on his behalf. It was a genuine draft, as the Piochers were adamant in their demand of placing the county funds in their home-town bank. Lee was reluctant to run against a fellow Democrat and a long-time friend, but his neighbors reminded him of his duty to the northern part of the county to run. In the three-man race, Clark and Lee were regarded as co-favorites, with the incumbent possessing a slight edge.

In Las Vegas, Lee's candidacy was said to have two objectives in view, "aside from the insatiable desire to draw salary. The first is to defeat the the county division movement and therefore maintain the same old crowd in office. The second object is to put themselves in position to juggle the county funds." The pro-Lee Searchlight *Bulletin* replied that "the first of these reasons is foolish, the second libelous."

The north thus turned the non-partisan county division issue into a partisan one within the race for office of county treasurer. Pioche and Searchlight believed that the "modest little community"

Las Vegas wanted nothing except "that cream of everything," and that the re-election of "handsome Edward, the watchdog of the treasury" meant two more years of rank favoritism.

To Las Vegans there was but one issue—county division. To the north, Lee's election was paramount. Because of intense campaigning, the Searchlight *Bulletin* reported that Lee was gaining on Clark: "Alkali from Las Vegas, gumbo from Caliente, and gravel from Pioche, the whole well-watered into political mud, had been heaved at Henry Lee, but like raw sugar, he has emerged from the treatment with his character the whiter and his issue the more refined in the eyes of the voters of Lincoln County."

Las Vegans generally believed that only a few from Pioche who had direct interests in the bank there were boosting Lee's candidacy. The editor of the *Age* viewed Lee with a suspicious eye, wondering if handling county funds was worth more to him than his old job of county recorder, as the salary for the position he had left was nearly double that of treasurer.

Campaigning in 1908 climaxed on election day with northern independent candidate Henry Lee defeating Clark. Lee won every northern precinct, as well as Searchlight in the south, as that anti-division stronghold gave him a splendid vote, 122 to 71. Ed Clark captured only one large town, Las Vegas, where he won big—233 to 21. One of the new treasurer's initial acts after being sworn in was to remove all county funds from Las Vegas to the bank in Pioche.

But Las Vegans had a right to be jubilant, too. Most winning candidates favored county division. Even Lee thought that it was inevitable, but he disapproved of Las Vegas' tactics of cramming the division scheme down the people's throat. The *Age* issued a new battle cry: "We must now get to work in carrying the county division campaign to a successful ending."

With county division assured, the Pioche *Record* in sheer desperation wondered why the seat of the new county should be in Las Vegas, as a few year's time might bring about a vast population increase at Searchlight. "It would make far and away the most beautiful county seat in the state."

"How does Overton feel?" further inquired the *Record*, which described that garden spot as a lusty rapidly maturing youth. The editor felt that the Clark County seat location should not be decided upon immediately, "lest some town might discover that its birthright had been sold for a mess of pot-

Henry H. Lee became an independent candidate for treasurer with the backing of the northern part of Lincoln County. Underlying his candidacy was the larger issue of county division. By upending Clark, Lee defeated a political giant in a classic battle.

tage." The jealous editor did not want to see rapidly developing Las Vegas gain additional prestige.

In January 1909 the Lincoln County Division Club carried its case directly to the state legislature. Late that same month a Lincoln County assemblyman introduced a bill to divide the county, and Las Vegans confidently looked for early action. The lawmakers were sympathetic, and Governor Denver S. Dickerson signed the bill creating Clark County on the evening of February 5. The new entity would come into existence on July 1, 1909.

The bill provided that Lincoln County's indebtedness would be divided between the two counties in proportion to their assessed valuations. Thus

Clark County would start its life with an indebtedness of about $430,000, its share of the $630,000 debt. Moreover, Clark would have no money or county property. This was a bitter pill, but county division was worth it.

Instead of scattering county offices throughout town, Las Vegas businessmen had pledged funds for temporary quarters even before the division bill became law. That spring a committee of the Division Club raised $1800 to construct a building on the Carson Street side of the courthouse square.

Las Vegas businessmen during June eagerly awaited the new county, and planned a "blowout" that would eclipse any ever held in Nevada. Four years of hopes and political maneuvering materialized on the morning of July 1. The ringing of bells, the booming of cannons, the popping of fireworks and other assorted noises greeted the birth of Clark County.

The day began at 4. a.m. with a national salute and band music. At 10 a.m. oratorical bombasts by civic leaders preceded the introduction of new county officials, who added their own predictions of a glorious future for the new county. Juvenile sports and races, a baseball game between Goodsprings and Las Vegas, hose fights, a burro race, a wheel barrow race, and an open-air band concert highlighted the afternoon. The festivities concluded that evening with a ball at the opera house.

On July 3, the Clark County commissioners held their first meeting in the new temporary courthouse, just completed. There was no jail, but Lincoln County agreed to accept prisoners from Clark County at $1.25 a day. Construction of a permanent building in the middle of the courthouse square did not begin until 1914, nearly five years later. The county accepted the $50,000 building on October 10, after its final payment, according to contract.

From the month of its founding, Las Vegas was desirous of joining the inner circle of Nevada county seat towns. A square block of the townsite had been set aside for county use. Beginning in July 1909 the humble block structure (above) on the north side of the courthouse square housed the county government until a two-story cement building (opposite page) with marble lined corridors was built in the center of the courthouse square. The old building then served several purposes, as Las Vegas City Hall and City Library combined into the 1940's, then as Library only before its removal around 1952. The larger courthouse gave way in 1960 to a multi-storied structure, which within a decade had to be expanded to meet county growth.

After this building's completion in 1914, the tree-shaded lawn furnished a cool retreat for Las Vegans on hot afternoons. Public meetings, especially political, were held on the steps with most of the audience comfortably seated on the grass.

Late in 1906 or early 1907 a photographer ascended a telephone pole and took this general view (below) of the San Pedro, Los Angeles & Salt Lake Railroad yards. Thirty-five of its engines and seven of the Las Vegas & Tonopah Railroad made this place an intermittent home. For the SP, LA & SL, Las Vegas was the division point between the coal burning engines running north and south. In the center of the picture is a fifty-ton capacity ice house that burned in the summer of 1907, resulting in Las Vegas' first calamity. Above is the machine shop with engine 22 on the turntable facing the roundhouse, after 1910.

CHAPTER SEVEN

Las Vegas' Later Years

FROM ITS FOUNDING IN 1905 LAS VEGAS REMAINED distinctly a railroad town until the building of Hoover (or Boulder) Dam after 1930. Until then railroad people heavily influenced the town's economic, political and social life.

Early in 1909, the same year that Las Vegas won the seat of Clark County, important news broke out that solidified the town's image as a railroad center. In bold headlines the Las Vegas *Age* announced that the San Pedro, Los Angeles and Salt Lake Railroad would proceed with building large machine and maintenance shops on the west edge of town. Senator William Clark and others of the railroad executive board in New York signed the order authorizing an initial outlay of $400,000 for the work. The facilities would employ up to 500 additional men, but in all the town's population would increase by 1200 to 1500.

Construction started on the shops during the first week of spring. Large plows began tearing up the sage-covered earth, creating great dust clouds. Scrapers smoothed several acres in preparation for digging the foundations of immense new buildings. Old freight cars became kitchens and bunkhouses for use by more than a hundred busy construction workers. The regular railroad employees moved into better quarters that summer after 65 handsome concrete cottages were finished in the original townsite.

This new prosperity and optimism for the future of Las Vegas ended dramatically on January 1, 1910, when a distant flood halted the trains and curtailed the town's commercial activity. An unseasonably warm rain on that New Year's Day caused rapid melting of a heavy snow-pack on mountains in Lincoln County. Flood waters swept through the narrow gap of Meadow Valley Wash, wiping out the rails and roadbed. Although most of the Southwest was affected by that disastrous winter storm, Meadow Valley Wash, with a drainage basin as large as many Eastern states, suffered the greatest damage.

Nearly a hundred miles of track, from a point north of Moapa to 36 miles north of Caliente, were destroyed. Thousands of railroad ties and great timbers from expensive bridges, as well as portions of ranch buildings, were carried for miles by the torrent. One freight train had proceeded only 15 miles south of Caliente before the flood overtook it. Though every car was washed away, all of the crew escaped by taking to the hills. The rain-drenched trainmen tramped through the mountains without food for nearly fifty exhausting miles before reaching help.

An eastbound train, the Los Angeles Limited which had left Las Vegas on December 31, did not reach Utah until mid-May. During the interim railroad men of the Salt Lake route deserted Las Vegas, except a skeleton crew to operate trains to Los Angeles, and payrolls dwindled to a minimum. Las Vegas businessmen had hard times until through traffic resumed on June 12. When the 1910 census was taken, Las Vegas' population was listed at only about 800.

That same summer construction began on a fine $25,000 grammar school on railroad-donated land bounded by Lewis and Bridger Avenues and Fourth and Fifth Streets. The modern federal courthouse now occupies the site. Because of numerous delays the building was not ready for occupancy

By the spring of 1909 Las Vegas was taking on a more stable appearance. It had more than ten miles of graded, oiled and curbed streets, imposing commercial buildings and other evidence of material growth. On the far right in the above picture is the mission-style railroad depot; the forest of steel columns and the skeletal structure to its left mark the partly constructed machine shops of the SP, LA & SL Railroad. The low building between it and the burning oil tank, is the round house. The corner further left is at First and Fremont Streets, where on opposite corners the Thomas Department store and the Ferron and Martin drug store were housed in brick and cement block buildings. Appearing above them on Main Street is the Armour ice plant operated by the Las Vegas Ice and Manufacturing Company. From its roof the railroad yards panorama (below) was taken. Extending out of the ice

plant in the lower right corner is the north end of a 900 foot loading platform which had a capacity to ice twenty refrigerated cars at a time. Further beyond are the machine shops in a building 150 by 380 feet built of massive concrete blocks. Between it and the stack is the power plant which until about 1930 generated electricity for both the shops and the town. Still further left is the roundhouse. Those facilities stabilized Las Vegas until the Hoover Dam era. On the unloading ramp at the far left, oil tankers were run up to discharge oil by gravity flow into the large storage tank. In the background the desert stretches westward through an area that was heavily developed in later years with a freeway, business districts and housing developments. The skyline shows Gass peak and the Sheep range beyond the north end of Las Vegas Valley.

Destruction of the first ice plant (shown on page 112) early one evening in July 1907 worked a hardship on the city until the 100-ton modern plant of reinforced concrete on the opposite page began to function later in the year. It was one of the Southwest's largest and the only icing station between San Bernardino and Salt Lake City, furnishing ice to stations all along the line. The plant also supplied local saloons. Iced punch sipped in the draft of an electric fan made a temperature of 112 degrees bearable.

The picture below, a near continuation of the large panorama on the preceding page, shows the south side of Las Vegas in 1911 with Sunrise (Frenchman) Mountain in the background. Below it is the combination grade and high school; to its left in downtown at Third and Bridger Streets is the Methodist Church with its steeple in plain view. To the left of the stack on Main Street is a series of warehouses owned by the Clark Forwarding Company. Neat rows of railroad built cottages for its working personnel are on the right side of the picture.

Bounteous water made Las Vegas the City of Destiny. Prominent early Las Vegans are shown in these views of artesian wells. From the left (below) are Peter Buol, who became the first Mayor of Las Vegas, Joe Ronnow and Bill Price. On the opposite page, from the left are Edmund W. Griffith, W. R. Thomas and John S. Park.

LAS VEGAS

"THE CITY OF DESTINY"

WHAT SHE IS AND HAS:

County Seat of Clark County.

Population 1,250. Age four years.

The Gateway to the Southern Nevada Mining Districts
— the richest on earth.

Division point on main line of Salt Lake Route.

Southern terminus of Las Vegas & Tonopah Railroad.

The main shops of Salt Lake System (now building).

Handsome Business Blocks of brick and cement.

First State Bank—one of the most substantial financial
institutions in the state.

Ice Factory—largest and finest in Nevada.

Six good Hotels and several lodging houses.

Handsome Opera House.

Numerous Fraternal Societies.

Electric Light Plant.

Modern Telephone Exchange.

Graded Schools and High School.

Two handsome Churches.

Ten miles of graded and curbed streets.

Pure Spring Water under pressure, piped to every lot.

The Las Vegas Promotion Society ("Has Nothing to Sell")

A set of live, up-to-date business men, conducting, among
other things:—

    General Merchandise Stores (5)——Clothing (4)
——Cigars and Confectionery (3) —— Hardware (1)——Millinery and Ladies' Wear (1)——
Drugs (1)——Barber Shops (3)——Meat Markets (2)——Bakery (1)——Restaurants (6)——
Plumbing Shop (1)——Blacksmith Shop (1)——
Moving Picture Show (1)——Attorneys (5)——
Physicians (2)——Dentists (2)——Billiard Halls
(2)——Bars and Saloons (11)——Newspapers (2)

Several Fine Ranches under cultivation.

——AND BEST OF ALL——
200,000 ACRES OF FERTILE LAND

With an inexhaustible supply of artesian water to irrigate it, waiting to produce every variety of fruits and vegetables, alfalfa, grain or anything a successful farmer would desire, with a splendid local market at top prices for the products.

until the fall of 1911. In the interim fire destroyed the old school, so temporary quarters had to be set up in the Methodist church and in an adjacent building.

The extensive railroad shops were placed into operation in January 1911. But the biggest news that year was town incorporation, provided in a legislative bill which Governor Tasker Oddie signed into law on March 16, 1911. It provided that Las Vegas would be governed by a mayor and a board of four commissioners, the first Nevada town to adopt that form of government which the City of Galveston, Texas popularized.

At a special election on June 1 Las Vegans approved the charter by 168 to 57. Peter Buol became mayor by the decisive margin of 35. The first commissioners were W. J. Stewart, Ed Von Tobel, C. M. McGovern, and J. J. Coughlin. It then became possible to issue sewer bonds, and later the electorate approved a $40,000 issue to install badly needed services.

Throughout the valley homesteads of ranches and small farms flourished. Development was naturally slow because it took nearly a year to uproot mesquite and sagebrush and prepare the ground for cultivation. A well had to be sunk to provide for irrigation, as rainfall was insufficient for farming. The lucky landowners had drilled their wells in the artesian belt of the valley, so that the water bubbled like a fountain on the surface and required no pumping.

Excellent farming results usually began with the second season. Except for citrus, many types of fruit, as well as grains and vegetables, were produced. In this valley of abundant water and favorable climate, alfalfa was one of the staple crops with up to six cuttings annually. Total production would reach eight to ten tons per acre for the season. One enthusiastic report stated that radishes matured in 18 days and that the largest apricot tree in the world grew at Las Vegas!

In Paradise Valley south of Las Vegas, where several downtown businessmen maintained holdings, ranches and farms successfully grew fruit trees, grain, hay, vegetables, and grapes. A few tried to grow cotton, and some plants grew three feet high with well-filled bolls.

World War I had virtually no permanent effect on the local economy. Through that decade and the next one Las Vegas remained an unimposing desert town surrounded by vast wastes and emptiness. Prospects of additional growth seemed very slim, indeed. But beginning in 1920 there were exciting rumors of dam construction on the Colorado River. The seven states of the Colorado River Basin set up a special commission to bring about what became Hoover Dam, named for the commission chairman and later U.S. President. Congress passed the Boulder Canyon Project Act (The Swing-Johnson bill) on December 21, 1928, and President Hoover signed the initial appropriation bill on July 3, 1930.

When the latter bill became law, the railroad shop whistle let go in one continuous scream, sending the whole town into a hysterical impromptu celebration. All businesses closed, except for the speakeasies, and Fremont Street was a mass of excited humanity. People who had not spoken for years became friends again. Ten long years of disappointment had stored up an emotional potential that seemed to be released all at once. The first appropriation meant that the U.S. Department of the Interior could proceed with dam construction.

Notable in the long fight for passage of these bills were Nevada Congressman Sam Arentz, and its Senators Tasker Oddie and Key Pittman, especially the latter. In Las Vegas, James Cashman Sr., C.P. Squires and Ed W. Clark vigorously backed the plan. Arizona's Governor and Senators provided strong opposition. The massive project on the river kept Las Vegas lively during the terrible Depression. Its banking institutions, for instance, closed only one day during President Franklin Roosevelt's Bank Holiday.

Six great Western contractors had formed a new corporation, Six Companies, Inc., which bid approximately $48.8 million to build the dam. Black Canyon, with steep near-perpendicular walls more than 700 feet high, was selected as the dam site. Work on the dam proper started in 1931 but before any work could be done on it, several miles of new roads, a construction camp at the present Boulder City, three railroad segments from a point south of Las Vegas to the dam site, two cofferdams across the river, and water diversion tunnels through Black Canyon's walls all had to be built.

The government accepted the 726-foot high dam in March 1935, and President Roosevelt dedicated it on September 30. An estimated 20,000 people watched the ceremony while millions of others heard his remarks over the national radio networks. Afterward the President was driven through Fremont Street.

As dam construction forces left, many felt that Las Vegas would soon revert to its former condition of dullness. Others believed that the dam itself would become a major tourist attraction, encouraging a thriving resort hotel trade. A noted Los Angeles hotelman named Thomas Hull opened the "plush" El Rancho Vegas south of town in 1940.

Viewing the success of that venture, R. E. Griffith, a Texas theatre-chain owner, built the Last Frontier on the Los Angeles highway far out in the desert in 1943. In town Robert Brooks built the Nevada Biltmore, and Marion B. Hicks erected the El Cortez in the early 1940's. Both became popular gathering places, especially for Las Vegans and military personnel.

Next came the Flamingo in 1946, promoted by Bugsy Siegel. It also became popular, although its principal backer was dramatically assassinated in Los Angeles. A year later Marion Hicks and Clifford A. Jones founded the Thunderbird Hotel—another success. Each hotel had a casino with the usual variety of gambling which had been legalized in 1931.

In addition to the advent of ranch-style resort hotels, two other major factors brought about by World War II combined to stimulate a boom and a population surge at Las Vegas. One development was the opening of Las Vegas Army Air Field at the present Nellis Air Force Base, nine miles north of town, in the spring of 1941.

That year the site, called McCarran Airfield, had only a Western Air Express dirt runway, a few shacks and a well. But soon a complex of buildings was constructed to train aerial gunners and qualify them for combat duty both in Europe and in the Pacific. The mission soon expanded to include training co-pilots for B-17's and B-29's. At the height of wartime operations the Base housed several thousand personnel.

Deactivation came in January 1947, and the base remained closed until it reopened as a fighter training school in 1949. In that year the base also received its present name, honoring a native Nevadan who lost his life in European combat. Nellis Air Force Base now trains pilots in all phases of fighter gunnery, rocketry and dive bombing.

The building of the mammoth $150 million complex of Basic Magnesium Incorporated in 1941 also provided a major economic boost during World War II. Refined brucite ore was hauled in by huge trucks from Gabbs, Nevada, 330 miles northwest, to feed the plant. By the time production started on August 31, 1942, a townsite named Henderson was laid out in the shadeless desert below Black Mountain.

Basic Magnesium quickly became the largest national manufacturer of metallic magnesium, then hailed as a miracle product used in making airplanes and aero engine parts. Its most important wartime role was production of magnesium for incendiary bombs dropped by Allied pilots on enemy war plants. The quick intense heat resulting from such bombs made fire control almost impossible and aided in crippling Germany's war machine.

After the war BMI suspended operations, and Henderson almost became a ghost town. But the Nevada legislature rescued the BMI plant in 1947 to reactivate it the next year as a the nucleus for several smaller peacetime industrial units. By the 1960's such nationally known chemical industrial producing firms as Stauffer Chemical Company, American Potash and Chemical Company, Montrose Chemical Company, and other firms such as Titanium Metals Corporation and Flintkote Company (producers of lime products) were using the original BMI plant units.

A mild climate allowing fishing and boating on Lakes Mead and Mohave also lured tourists and permanent residents. The many factors allowing the new growth upped Las Vegas' population in 1950 to 24,624, a substantial increase from the 8,422 recorded a decade earlier.

Resort hotel and casino building continued early in the new decade. In 1950 Wilbur Clark opened his sumptuous Desert Inn Hotel, and two years later Milton Prell followed with the Sahara, on the site of the old Club Bingo. The Sands appeared in 1953, and early the next year came the nine-story Riviera Hotel, the first one to abandon the low ranch style spreading over many acres. A strip of hotels evolved that made Las Vegas distinctive from Reno. Each new resort brought a new line of patronage and additional fame to the city.

About that same time William J. Moore, Jr. founded the Showboat Hotel in 1954, not on the Strip but on the Boulder Highway. In West Las Vegas The Moulin Rouge was built in 1955. In the heart of downtown Las Vegas, the Fremont Hotel opened in 1956 as a high rise towering over a gambling district then called Glitter Gulch. The oldest club on Fremont Street was the Boulder Club, which had opened its doors in 1930 soon after Congress had approved funds for the dam. Other clubs followed, and the Golden Nugget was opened soon after World War II, in 1946. The Apache Hotel ultimately developed into the Horseshoe Club under Benny Binion. The Lucky Strike, the Bingo Club, the Pioneer, the Westerner, the California Club, the Monte Carlo, and the Las Vegas Club were other notable downtown casinos.

In the late 1950's the Las Vegas Strip experienced another round of expensive hotel building when the Dunes, the Hacienda, the Tropicana and the Stardust opened their doors in successive years beginning in 1955. As a result the population of Las Vegas surged to 64,406 in 1960. The area population was approximately 119,200.

The remarkable growth of the 1950's was also aided by the development of atomic testing at the huge Nevada Test Site, sixty miles northwest of Las Vegas. Beginning on January 27, 1951, the U.S. Atomic Energy Commission began a series of 45 nuclear tests and development of experimental devices during the next 4½ years. Yields ranged in size from less than a kiloton, or 1000 tons of TNT, up to somewhat less than a hundred kilotons.

An adjacent 90,000 acre test area, the Nuclear Rocket Development Station built in 1957 at Jackass Flats, tested nuclear powered rockets. Both facilities provided employment for thousands, resulting in the founding of the town of Mercury at the site and the expansion of Indian Springs Air Force Auxiliary Field. The nuclear testing made important contributions to atomic energy in developing defense weapons, rockets for use in outer space and in various peacetime uses.

During the 1960's hotel construction continued with abandon both downtown and on the Strip, creating an urbane atmosphere and a sophisticated skyline. The Mint Hotel built in downtown Las Vegas in 1964 was joined by the Four Queens two years later. In that same year Caesars Palace opened on the Strip. The Frontier Hotel followed a year later. Two additional hotels—the Landmark and the Las Vegas Hilton—opened in 1969 on boulevards adjacent to the existing Strip, marking the first time that hotels not on Las Vegas Boulevard South were considered part of the Strip. These new hotels and smaller resorts such as the Castaways, built in 1963, and the Aladdin in 1966 all brought growth in gaming and resort industries.

In 1971 the Union Plaza Hotel opened at the head of Casino Center. There was talk of additional hotel construction. Behind the mask of the Strip is an air-conditioned town made up of substantial citizens who seldom if ever gamble, but occasionally spend an evening enjoying the unparalleled entertainment that the town offers.

These Las Vegans comprise a community with its own social, educational, cultural and recreational activities which combine for worthwhile family living in this hot dry climate. They enjoy boating and skiing and other outdoor sports. They read books, attend churches, take in the movies and go on weekend vacations. They do anything that a family might in Seattle or Boston. Underneath the glamor and tinsel of Las Vegas is a normal American city that continues to grow, maintaining a character only seen by visitors who linger awhile.

121

Early in July 1905 Ed W. Clark arrived in Las Vegas to set up the tent store shown on the top of the opposite page. Merchandise soon overflowed those canvas warehouses, and so Clark and a new partner, C. C. Ronnow (at right in the above interior view) built a wood-frame store on South Main Street. The men were forwarding agents for freight by horse and mule teams to area mining camps, especially to Rhyolite until a railroad was built to there in 1906. The store in 1906 had the best variety in town. In the glass case at left are bridle bits, egg beaters, hay hooks, strap razors, sharp pocket knives, pocket combs and large pipes. On the walls from the left to the right are shoes, dishes, pots and pans, overalls, work socks, collar pads for horses (behind Ira Earl at far left), tobacco, canned goods and toilet paper for the elite. In the wooden boxes on the floor are dried staples which were weighed in the scales. An old fashioned coffee mill is at the far end of the counter.

On the roof of his wood frame store (below), Ronnow installed a solar water system to provide hot water. Pipes were laid back and forth under glass, and water was circulated through them. Two young trees are boxed to prevent burros from eating the bark. Between them is a "Mormon" slip-scraper, a one-man earth remover. Note also the water barrels on the front porch of the store.

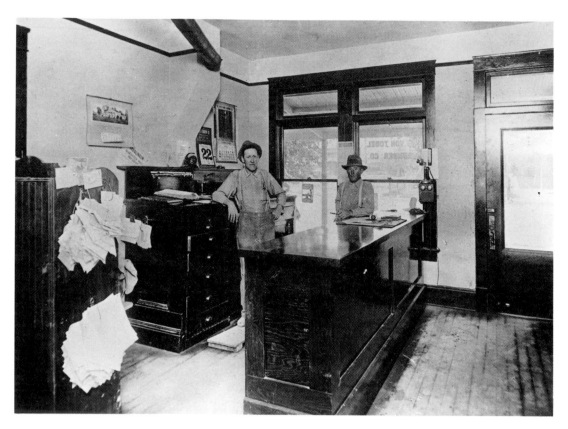

Ed Von Tobel, Sr. came to Las Vegas on the train in 1905, bought two lots at auction, and a month later opened a lumber yard on the 500 block on South Main Street. That location soon proved to be too far out of town, and he moved in closer to Fremont on South First Street, as shown in the bottom picture. Shingles are stacked high at left behind the wagon, and the proprietor is in the middle. A 1914 fire destroyed the building. In the rebuilt office (above) Von Tobel stands on a spring board to give him added height to work at the bookkeeper's desk. Note the chimney for an old wood stove; wooden boxes and scrap lumber were used for fuel. The invoice department is at left where papers are hap-hazardly spiked on the side of the cabinet. The early style telephone is in an inconvenient location; there were not more than 250 phones in Las Vegas around World War I. From these humble beginnings the Ed Von Tobel Lumber Company has evolved into an ultra-modern building materials department store and lumber yard in a 90,000 square foot building.

From modest beginnings in 1905 on South First Street (above) the Clayson & Griffith store moved a year later to a block building on Fremont Street. They sold all types of general merchandise including explosives. Edmund W. Griffith, who originally came here to build the roundhouse, also rented and sold burros which he found in the nearby deserts. He also went as far away as Baja, California to procure animals. Later a president of the Chamber of Commerce, Griffith once said, "I take care of five acres in Las Vegas and five acres will take care of you." His son, Robert, has carried on the same spirit of boosting Las Vegas, engaging in a number of enterprises.

BANISH BURROS

STRAYS MUST BE IMPOUNDED

Energetic and United Effort Will Clear the City

With regard to the bands of stray burros which infest our City, the Age publishes the following statement on the subject by E. W. Griffith of the firm of Clayson & Griffith.

"We have been engaged in dealing inb urros for the use of prospectors. in connection with our mining supply business in this city. We have endeavored at all times to keep our band of burros entirely away from town, most of the time having them located about five miles from here, north of the Kyle ranch. Whenever our band has approached the town we have employed men to drive them back. Nearly all the stray animals now about the town have been turned loose and left by prospectors. We are heartily in favor of keeping the town absolutely free from stray stock and if there is a move in that direction will see to it that none of our burros are allowed to roam the streets.

We are also heart and soul in favor of a tree planting campaign, and will give it all possible encouragement.

We have now had enough experiance to know what trees will do well in this locality, and I believe the general planting of trees at this time will result in inestimable benefit to the town."

E. W. GRIFFITH.

F. W. Manuel, Night Police and Fire Marshall, says that under the present conditions it is impossible to impound all stray animals, as there is no place to keep them. That he has recommended to the Town Trustees that a proper place be provided for this purpose, and in the mean time, is keeping as many as possible in yard of the jail. Also that it is difficult to sell these impounded animals for enough to pay for feeding them the required ten days.

This matter having been brought to the attention of the Board of Town Trustees at their meeting Friday morning at 11:00, it was recommended to the County Commissioners that funds be set aside at once for the purpose of providing a city pound.

Let us hope and pray.

Ever since its opening in a rough lumber building shown in the previous chapter, the Arizona Club had prospered. In March 1906 it moved into these spacious mission-style quarters which had elaborately curved windows of leaded, beveled plate glass and matching front doors of solid oak. Concrete blocks made in downtown Las Vegas were used to build the exterior walls. Around 1907 Al James, third from the right on the opposite page, acquired the Arizona Club from its builder James O. McIntosh and added a second story with red-light features. The upstairs was regarded as the "niftiest house of joy on the Pacific Coast." The interior finish was of quartered oak with pink Tennessee marble baseboards. The club's crowning glory was the $23,000 thirty-foot long mahogany bar with an elaborately designed back-bar of imported French plate glass of optic design. Later both the bar and glass front entrance became part of the Last Frontier Hotel's Horn Room. Railroad passengers of that early era ran a well-worn path to quaff its fine beer and whiskey, while railroad crews serviced or changed engines in the yards.

On the upper floor of the Thomas Department Store's cement block building at First and Fremont Streets was the town's opera house. Socials and dances also were held there. J. F. Miller's Hotel Nevada (below) eventually evolved into the modern Sal Sagev at Main and Fremont Streets. From Beatty, Miller rode into town in a buggy similar to the one shown here and opened this concrete hotel in January 1906, when this picture was taken.

At the dawn of 1906 the First State Bank at First and Fremont Streets, threw open its doors to display its marble floor and mahogany fixtures to the banking public. Its founder, John S. Park is in the cashier's cage. The exterior (above) built of hollow concrete blocks was shaded by a colonnaded portico. Originally established before the opening of Las Vegas townsite, the First State Bank remained a substantial financial institution for many decades, helping to develop the town by investing in untold numbers of homes and business improvements. In 1957 this building was razed to make way for a casino.

In 1905 newspapers reported that Senator William Clark would build a $300,000 sanitorium at Las Vegas. After the townsite opened up Dr. Roy W. Martin established a private hospital which may have been in the top building at left. The railroad also had a hospital on First Street.

A view of the Las Vegas skyline in 1910 (below) does not disclose a great number of steeples. Built in 1908, the Methodist church at Third and Bridger Streets with its spiral is shown to the left of the Episcopal church, organized in the fall of 1907. Further right and closer to the camera is the Las Vegas fire house with its bell clearly shown. That building would be in back of the present Horseshoe Club. A closeup of the Methodist church and parsonage is at middle left, while a later view of the Episcopal church with nearby residences is on the top of the opposite page.

In the middle of the Fremont Street business district (left) around Christmastime in 1916 the town's citizens placed a tree with multicolored lights. Beyond the First State Bank and Ferron's Drug Store is the Overland Hotel. The grocery store pictured below is opposite the bank.

As early as 1908 Las Vegas had a theatre. Others followed, and at Third and Fremont Streets after World War I, Cragin and Pike opened the airdome (opposite page), a type of theatre common in the desert country. Though a high board fence enclosed it, impecunious children climbed the umbrella trees to watch a free show. The movies were well attended especially in the summer because entertainment was scarce while Las Vegans waited until about midnight for the night to cool off sufficiently to go to sleep. In the late 1920's the outdoor theatre gave way to the El Portal, shown at bottom under construction. "Talkies" were shown there for the first time in 1929.

Above is Fremont Street looking east, about 1925

Below is Fremont Street looking west, about 1925.

After establishing a one-owner, one-employee automobile business, in the gold mining community of Searchlight, Nevada, James Cashman moved to Las Vegas in 1920 to set up shop on Main Street, around the corner from Fremont Street, shown at right. Showrooms were on the left side of the Overland Hotel building, whose lobby is behind the umbrella trees on the right side. In 1941 Cashman built modern showrooms across Main Street on its west side, where he sold cars and trucks until the early 1970's.

Fremont Street around 1920 was a busy dirt and gravel thoroughfare where the dust hung low, especially on hot summer days. Without air conditioning, cars were like ovens on wheels. At the head of the street is the mission-style Union Pacific depot (formerly the San Pedro, Los Angeles & Salt Lake Railroad). Five through passenger trains ran to Los Angeles daily in the mid-1920's. The buff colored walls of the depot (below) contrast with the terra cotta tile roofing. At right is the waiting room. Downstairs in the center is the well-ventilated ticket office. Amid the trees at the far left was the "Beanery", a popular restaurant for locals. Behind the building a broad circle driveway leads to the intersection of Main and Fremont Streets. The improved grounds had extensive flower beds and trees, restful sights for the train-weary traveler. In 1940 it was razed to make way for a modern depot.

J. W. Garehime's music store opened in 1924 on Fremont Street and initially sold jewelry as well. California supply houses let the firm have band and brass instruments on consignment. The store also carried upright Starr pianos at $420, banjos, Victrolas, sheet music, piano rolls and popular Edison and Victor wind-up "gramaphones".
A fair selection of thick ten-inch wide records was also available. The proprietor is flanked by two Hollywood comedians playing instruments ordered for the local Eagles Lodge. In 1941 the firm moved to North Third Street and finally in 1965 into a modern building on East Sahara Avenue.

Probably Las Vegas' finest restaurant in the 1920's, the Oasis was a popular gathering place where the town's elite spent sociable dinner hours. Pretty little Mormon girls from the rural areas served as waitresses. Late in the evening movie goers left the airdome for a big ice cream sundae here. With a small dance floor and music, high-schoolers often finished a date here by investing a nickel in the juke box and a dime in ice cream sodas.

Below is the first floor of the Griffith building at Second and Fremont Streets, among Las Vegas' finest until about 1930. Professional offices are upstairs, and the post office is on the corner.

When this $35,000 combination grammar and high school (the center building in the picture below) was built on railroad donated land in 1911, many pessimists scorned the expenditure, believing that Las Vegas never would have enough children to fill the classrooms. The two-story mission-style building had modern features including a heating plant and electric fan ventilation. After Las Vegas High School was built at Seventh and Bridger Street in 1929, this became Fifth Street Grammar School.

Classes were dismissed at the end of the second week in May because of the heat. The time was made up by limiting Easter vacation to Good Friday and Christmas vacation to the week between Christmas and New Year's. Beginning in the mid-1930's, when the annual Helldorado was begun, Elks Lodge officials (above) conducted a children's party at the school. Note the old-time fiddler and square dance caller in the foreground.

From its first year, Las Vegas had fire protection provided by a volunteer fire department. Initially, when there was a fire, anyone with a gun would run into the street and shoot into the air. Later a four-foot triangle at First and Fremont was rung to summon the Las Vegas volunteer fire department. The fire company then used a buckboard with a hose rolled up in a coil and other vehicles before finally around 1920 acquiring a modern truck with ladders and hand extinguishers. Its members served with honor and distinction, providing excellent service until a regular department took their place around 1940.

The Rotary Club of Las Vegas boasted a membership of prominent Las Vegans in the early 1930's. In the bottom row, from the left are Ernie Cragin, Bill Beckley, Fred Hesse, O. C. Boggs, Jim Cashman, O. K. Adcock, Mel Riley, William Ferron, a Rotary guest, C. E. Pembroke, and Sam J. Lawson. In the top row, from the left are Dr. William S. Park, Dr. Forest Mildren, William Pike, A. A. Hinman, Harry Anderson, Dr. Roy W. Martin, C. P. "Pop" Squires, Jack Heaton, Harry Blanding, Charlie Ronnow, Cyril Wengert, Ed W. Clark, E. W. Griffith, W. N. Schuyler, and Walter Bracken.

In the 1920's airplanes landed at Rockwell Airport off Las Vegas Boulevard south of the Sahara Hotel. From the airport truck (below) an airport employee is hand-pumping gasoline into the tank of a Western Air Express Douglas M-2. This sturdy biplane which arrived April 17, 1926, initiated regularly scheduled service between Los Angeles and Salt Lake City via Las Vegas. Note the cache which gives additional particulars. On the outgoing plane (top opposite page) horseman Bill Morgan delivers the first bag of air mail to pilot Fred Kelly before he climbed into the clear Nevada sky. The bottom pictures show side views of a World War I fighter plane and the front end of a Douglas M-2 with its liquid cooled radiator.

1880-1926
Las Vegas Nev April 17 '26

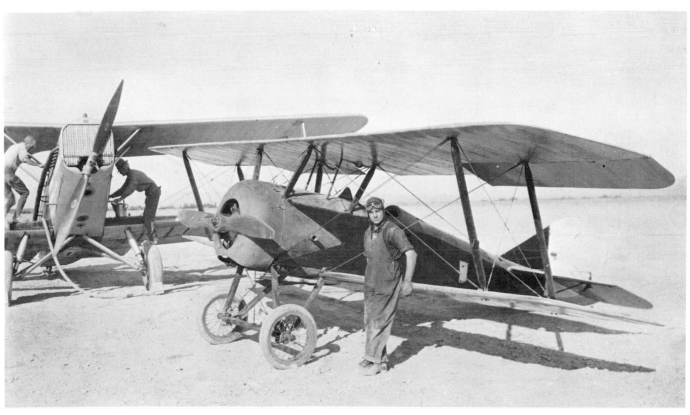

Crude in the extreme were early Las Vegas gas stations such as the one pictured above. In the 1930's Tower's Service Station was located on Fifth Street between Fremont and Carson Streets.

Dr. Roy W. Martin converted the Palace Hotel on North Second Street into a hospital. After he built the new Las Vegas hospital at Eighth and Ogden Streets, the old building became El Patio Hotel. No surgery was performed in the summer except emergency work at 4 or 5 a.m. Fans blowing over blocks of ice at floor level provided some coolness. Anyone who could wait a day was sent to California. Below is Rockwell's Electric shop in the 1930's. Leon Rockwell was a devoted collector of early Las Vegas relics, particularly Indian artifacts.

The Chamber of Commerce was established in 1911 to boost Las Vegas. In 1929 offices were on Fremont Street, as shown in the winter scene below. A list of past presidents reads like a **Who's Who** of Las Vegas. About that same year the local Boy Scouts posed in front of a famous sign that railroad passengers could see from their cars when in the station near the depot.

146

Favorite spots the year around during the 1920's and 1930's were the local swimming pools. Many preferred well-shaded Ladd's resort (above) near Twelfth Street. In a heavily developed residential area the Mermaid pool (below) on Fifth Street just north of Fremont was where many Las Vegans learned to swim. Many considered it fashionable because of its high fence.

Ward's Mesquite Grocery at First and Fremont Streets had a large delivery truck. Nobody left his store hungry, but unfortunately the proprietor went broke extending credit. Later when Ward (fourth from left) ran for justice of the peace, his old customers rallied around him and put him in with a big vote.

Between Fremont and Ogden Streets on North Main Street in the 1930's was the Troy Laundry, one of the first to employ steam facilities. It was noted for its fast delivery trucks.

In the 1930's rooms without bedding were only a dollar at the Gateway Auto Court, at Fifth Street and Charleston Blvd. This shaded oasis was the first glimpse of coolness to greet the weary tourist from California. Early in the Depression in 1931 Stanley M. Paher (Pahor) and his father, Gabriel, erected these Spanish tiled cabins with car ports. Large cottonwood trees shaded the motel until about 1960, when underground water levels fell and most of the trees died. It is still a well attended modern motel.

Around 1928-29, the Las Vegas Review-Journal operated out of a building on South First Street. Publisher Frank Garside, later city postmaster, is on the far left; beside him is Albert E. Cahlan, editor and co-publisher. The company car was used to deliver the evening papers. On the door is a poster showing the heralded Hoover (Boulder) Dam. The paper's masthead for awhile said, "Everybody knows Las Vegas is the best town by a damsite."

As the closest town to Hoover (Boulder) Dam construction, the somnolent desert village of Las Vegas early in 1929 quickly was transformed into a high-rolling boom town. Carloads of building materials passed through Las Vegas for transshipment to the dam site in Black Canyon, shown below a few years before construction began on the dam itself. Those imposing ramparts of black lava on the Colorado River were first visited by Army Lieutenant Joseph C. Ives in his sternwheeler, the Explorer. *He later wrote that each turn in the canyon "disclosed new combinations of colossal and fantastic forms, dimly seen in the dizzy heights overhead."*

In the downstream view (opposite page) taken late in 1932 or early 1933, diversion tunnels (not shown) were carrying water around the dam foundation site. About 900 feet below the tram is the lower coffer dam which prevented water from backing up into the excavation site. At that time the bedrock was being cleaned and allowed to dry thoroughly before actual construction got underway. High-scalers already had scraped the left (Arizona side) canyon wall to reach solid rock. The Nevada spillway is in the right foreground, and its lookout point is above the tram towers.

One of the world's greatest modern engineering projects, Hoover Dam was so gigantic in dimensions and vast in economic significance that its progress was followed world wide. The Bureau of Reclamation awarded the $49 million contract to build the dam to Six Companies, Incorporated, a combination of six different Western construction firms. In the above picture trains are hauling excavation muck out of Black Canyon to a point north of the damsite, while below one of the four huge diversion tunnels, the first major task in the project, is being built. Workmen are placing steel pipes and lining at the upper end of a tunnel. Pipes were rolled and welded near the site. Initially the tunnels merely diverted water past the dam site. Later the two nearest the Colorado River on either side were plugged with concrete when the power turbines were put into operation.

After water diversion was accomplished, the work of excavating approximately 5.8 million cubic yards of muck and gravel began in order to key to solid canyon rock the great wedge of 3.6 million yards of concrete. Bedrock was encountered in the spring of 1933. Beginning that same June, it took more than a year and a half of continuous twenty-four hour operations to pour the concrete. The giant honeycomb of alternating blocks of concrete and the later grouting produced one massive concrete obstacle which could withstand the tremendous pressure of Lake Mead.

On the opposite page the winter sun is just behind the completed dam, about noon. The black streak on the dam's face is the refrigerator slot containing an elaborate maze of pipes and valves which were used to circulate cool water through the setting concrete. The finishing touch to the dam was filling that slot with concrete. All four of the 390 foot intake towers built on the shelves of the canyon walls are shown, though not yet functioning because water was still going through the diversion tunnels in this 1935 view of the upstream face of the dam.

President Franklin D. Roosevelt dedicated the dam on September 30, 1935. Its completion meant different things to different communities: flood control for Imperial Valley, an increased domestic water supply for Southern California, power for mines and water control for irrigation in Arizona, and power for later industrial and commercial expansion of southern Nevada.

When Lake Mead formed behind the dam, boating and water sports came to the desert. A waterway for scenic wanderings developed to the lower end of the Grand Canyon, more than 115 miles upstream. The lake holds the silt-laden waters which pour out of the Grand Canyon.

While Hoover Dam was being constructed on the Colorado River, small night clubs opened in Las Vegas. Since the Bureau of Reclamation forbade gambling and liquor sales in Boulder City, single workers with the urge to gamble left their dormitories on weekends and emptied their pockets at Las Vegas establishments. At right, entertainers are advertising the Red Rooster, which was the first night club on the Los Angeles highway in an area that is now the fabulous Strip.

The Meadows was the scene of many gala parties. Located at the east end of Las Vegas near 25th Street, it was the town's first major supper club. Despite the Depression and prohibition, cheer for each New Year's Eve and all other occasions was present in copious quantities.

Hoover Dam gave Las Vegas gambling, legalized in 1931, an impetus toward greater and grander things. These clubs along Fremont Street, a drab section in the 1920's, developed in the 1930's into a Great White Way of casinos and saloons competing for public favor. New clubs had opened up beside enlarged older establishments by the late 1930's, when this picture was taken. The first one was the Boulder Club (below) which opened in 1929.

Mounted on the donkey (above) is the first queen of the annual Helldorado celebrations, Louise Di Fleour. To her left is deputy U. S. marshall Patrick Gallagher in a coonskin cap. Kneeling is newspaper editor John F. Cahlan, who helped promote many of the early celebrations. In the picture at right, Robert R. Russell registers Glen E. "Bud" Bodell and his burro at the Apache Hotel.

Before tourist interest in Hoover Dam developed in the mid-1930's, Las Vegans inaugurated in April 1935 the annual Helldorado celebration to attract visitors and provide entertainment for the locals. For more than a quarter of a century the four days of festive parading, broncho-busting and beard growing that made up Helldorado were an important part of Las Vegas' social calendar, but since about 1960 the celebration had taken a side seat to more modern forms of entertainment.

Most Helldorados had three major parades. Thursday's old timer's parade which featured only marching bands and historic animal-drawn vehicles was followed by the children's parade on Saturday, when every boy and girl in Las Vegas was either in the parade or lining the streets watching friends. On Sunday the beauty parade had numerous floats entered by Strip hotels and downtown clubs.

By the late 1930's a popular western sports event — a rodeo — was added to the celebration. A park adjacent to the downtown business section was converted to an arena. Cowboys from throughout the West challenged bucking broncs and Brahma bulls. The four-day rodeo became so popular that by 1948 the Elks Lodge of Las Vegas, Helldorado's principal sponsor, constructed Cashman field on North Fifth Street near the crest of a hill overlooking North Las Vegas.

Adjacent to Cashman field a Helldorado village ultimately was built by Las Vegans who volunteered their time and donated materials for a large amusement park. Robert B. Griffith gave logs and timber from his forest lands on Mount Charleston for buildings and a high stockade fence around the village.

Beards such as those worn by the men in the above bar scene were grown especially for Helldorado. On a given day weeks in advance, freshly shaven men began to grow beards that were judged for both length and style by pretty town girls with handy rulers. Helldorado was an outstanding example of city-wide cooperation in a community struggling for national recognition. Success came through pictures and stories published in metropolitan newspapers.

Gala scenes were the rule at early Helldorados. Above, a "prospector" deposits silver dollars at the First State Bank, while below various townspeople wear early western costumes at a drinking session in one of the downtown bars.

"Oh! Please, please! Don't hang my husband!" cries the wife of a man found guilty of the very serious crime of not wearing a western costume while on Fremont Street. He had been fined $500 and could not pay it, but a dollar bill soon would save him from a certain necktie party. This is part of Kangaroo Kourt, one of the most popular features of the old Helldorado. Visitors left disappointed if they did not get arrested and thrown into the old iron jail set up on Fremont Street. Though a semblance of the Kangaroo Court manages to live on, the real spirit of this horseplay regrettably departed Las Vegas about 1960.

A group of mid-1930's civic leaders (below) are in the Sal Sagev bar where Sid Martin served his famous sloe gin fizz. The men are collecting money in ten gallon hats to support the Helldorado.

Various businesses sponsored children's entries in the parade (top, opposite page). Below it is the "Desert Love Buggy," a 1904 Sears Roebuck automobile driven by James Cashman, a leading Helldorado organizer. In front of the vehicle a sign bears the town's slogan of the 1940's: "Still a Frontier Town."

In an early Helldorado rodeo scene (right) an onrushing bull makes the brave but cautious cowboys scurry up the fence of a bull pen. The Death Valley Express (below) passes by the former location of one of Nevada's largest department stores, Ronzone's. This entry in the old timer's parade carries early southern Nevadans including C. P. "Pop" Squires (attired in a checkered shirt and waving his hand) and David Farnsworth, who sits immediately behind Squires.

"Now take'er in like this" instructs a jet fighter training teacher in a pre-flight huddle with three other F-86 Sabre jet jockies at Nellis Air Force Base, at the north end of Las Vegas Valley. Beginning in 1941 fliers were trained for combat duty in just eight weeks before they entered the war zones. Below, a crew chief motions a McDonnell RF-101 Voodoo into position for a photo reconnaissance mission in 1962. The varied activity at Nellis Air Force Base, the industrial plants at Henderson (opposite page), and continued resort hotel building sustained Las Vegas through the 1940's.

The availability of land, water and power and a mild climate combined to attract Basic Magnesium Incorporated to this site halfway between Las Vegas and Boulder City in 1941. Soon red steel columns rose from the sage-covered sand which in 1942 were enclosed by asbestos-covered sheet-steel and concrete. Inside the buildings a fantastic assembly of furnaces, grinders, tanks, mixers, and countless other contraptions processed magnesium oxide into solid forms for wartime uses. Above are construction camps with dormitories, tents and commissary, while below access roads wind through shops and storage areas. Three of ten chlorine production units are at right.

In the 1940's Las Vegas had many establishments which attracted not only the sunburned men working at Basic Magnesium in Henderson and at Nellis Air Force Base, but also motorists traveling through the Southwest. Curious sightseers would refresh themselves at motels before taking a casual look at the various games and even courting Lady Luck. Beginning around 1943-1945 weekend Los Angelenos in significant numbers began to descend upon Las Vegas to sample the pleasures that the clubs offered. They came with such regularity that one man remarked. "Las Vegas is the greatest little California town in Nevada." In fact, it was virtually a suburb of Los Angeles.

At the various tables no social distinctions are observed; it is not uncommon to see a be-diamonded divorcee, a burly truck driver, a snappy dressed businessman and a construction worker all rubbing shoulders and tossing dice. In these mid-1940's views most men are wearing hats and there is only a sprinkling of women placing bets. The casinos never close their doors, prospering because of a multitude of small losers who have an urge to gamble.

The top two photos show the old game of faro, popular in the Western goldfields of Alaska and California. Players stake bets upon one or several cards by placing chips on a layout of a suit of spades covering the table. After the dealer closes the betting he deals a turn of two cards from a face up deck of cards encased in a small box with a slit in its side. The chances between the dealers and players are even. Basic odds in favor of the house improve with craps, third picture following. That game has many bewildering rules and is played on an elaborate layout. Glamorous roulette (bottom) is strictly a game of chance, not unlike faro in that respect.

Five stories high, the spectacular signs of Vegas Vic (opposite page) decked out in a broad brimmed hat, bandana and spurs, towers above the Pioneer Club. The swagger of his arms back and forth was visible all along Fremont Street and from the railroad depot. Astonished through passengers stood in amazement, fully assured that Las Vegas was no ordinary railroad stop.

When the first decade of legalized gambling ended in 1941, most of the gambling activity centered in a two-block area on Fremont Street. But the building of sprawling ranch style hotels on the Los Angeles highway leading south out of town soon changed the little desert town into an internationally celebrated resort and gambling center.

El Rancho Vegas which opened in 1941 ultimately had a swimming pool and dozens of bungalows amid landscaped grounds that included a waterfall running over native rocks. The "Come As You Are" spirit was at the sign of the windmill.

In 1942 important hotel interests bladed away the desert scrub growth and tumbleweeds two miles south of El Rancho Vegas and built the Hotel Last Frontier. Those two hotels and the others which would soon follow started a trend and initiated a boom at Las Vegas that soon surpassed the Hoover Dam growth of the 1930's. The top picture shows a mural in the Gay 90's Bar. At middle is the luxurious Ramona Room, whose walls contained stone laid by New Mexico Zuni Indians. The long low-style western exterior motif, as shown below, exemplifies the hotel's slogan, "The Early West in Modern Splendor." In this building the Hunt breakfast was served every Sunday, when Vegans gathered after church for what became a community social tradition.

Atomic testing changed the industrial face of Las Vegas after the Atomic Energy Commission set up the Nevada Test Site in January, 1951, sixty-five miles northwest of Las Vegas. In the next twenty years more than 300 underground nuclear tests helped develop weapons for national defense and peacetime purposes. Initially, several bombs were exploded aboveground; the photos below of one single shot were taken in a matter of seconds. The last picture at right dramatically shows the updraft of black dirt which has connected with the stem of the mushroom. Regional photographers wearing heavy lenses are taking photographs. Unconcerned about the radiation fallout, Las Vegans took the blasting at Yucca and Frenchman Flats in stride, and roulette wheels spun with hardly a tremor.

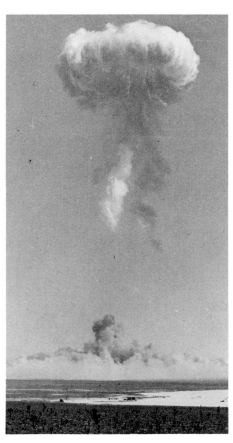

Bibliographic Essay

Books and manuscript sources available for research on Las Vegas history are very meager, indeed. No general history is available about the city, except for a brief chapter or two in books about gambling. No published biography has been accorded a Las Vegan. During most of the writing of this book, the author continually broke new ground in uncovering facts about Las Vegas and its earliest settlers.

Information in this book has come from extensive and varied sources. Oral interviews were held, and volumes of Southwestern newspapers and various manuscript materials, including letters, notes and diaries, were studied. What follows is by no means a complete list of authorities consulted. They are listed informally. Should an individual or an institution be interested in the source of any statement in this book, such information will be freely given in response to an inquiry sent to the author in care of the publisher.

CHAPTER ONE. The best single source of Spanish Trail material is the fifteen volume *Far West and Rockies Series* (1954-1961), compiled by Leroy and Ann Hafen. Volume One, "The Old Spanish Trail, Santa Fe to Los Angeles," contains many diaries including those of Antonio Armijo and Orville Pratt. Volume Two, "Journals of the Forty-Niners, Salt Lake to Los Angeles," has the diaries and records of many individuals who passed through Las Vegas enroute to California. In Volume Fifteen are supplementary journals of emigrants who describe Las Vegas Springs before 1855.

Other important diarists were S. N. Carvalho who offers area descriptions in his *Incidents of Travel in the Far West* (1857), and John C. Fremont who compiled a *Report of the Exploring Expedition to the Rocky Mountains in the Year 1842 and to Oregon and Northern California in the Years 1843-44.*

Among other books, William B. Rice's *The Los Angeles Star* (1947) has an Appendix containing an excellent footnoted document, "Early Freighting on the Salt Lake-San Bernardino Trail." *Overland with Kit Carson* (1930) by George D. Brewerton also proved to be useful. Escalante's travels adjacent to this area are in *Pageant in the Wilderness* (1950) by Herbert E. Bolton. Captain James H. Simpson's *Report of Explorations Across the Great Basin of the Territory of Utah* contains excellent Escalante material in its extended introduction.

Important newspaper references of the early 1850's are in the *Deseret News* which is published in Salt Lake City, the San Francisco *Alta* and the Los Angeles *Star*.

CHAPTER TWO. This section devoted to the Mormon mission rests heavily on original diaries of John Steele, Lorenzo Brown, and George W. Bean, all of which are in the Office of Historian, Church of Jesus Christ of Latter-Day Saints, in Salt Lake City. The "History of Las Vegas Mission" compiled by Andrew Jensen and preserved in the *Nevada Historical Society Papers, Volume V* (1926), is the most accessible and readable of the Mormon documents. Francis H. Leavitt's unpublished University of Nevada master's thesis, *The Influence of the Mormon People in the Settlement of Clark County*, (1934) makes good use of research materials available to him, though his conclusions show an overemphasis upon "Mormon influence." The *Deseret News* in 1855-1857 printed many interesting letters sent by the Las Vegas missionaries to Salt Lake City.

CHAPTER THREE. Details about the Potosi mine and Fort Baker in the early 1860's are hard to find. The little known story about those two places was pieced together after careful readings of the San Francisco *Alta*, Los Angeles *Star*, Los Angeles *Southern News*, Visalia *Delta*, San Francisco *Mirror*, and the Salt Lake City *Deseret News*. The best study of Fort Baker is "Carleton's Empty Fort" by George Rhulen in the *Nevada Historical Society Quarterly*, (Spring 1959).

CHAPTER FOUR. Personal information about Las Vegas Ranch and its founder Octavius D. Gass came from taped interviews with Fenton M. Gass at Bryn Mawr, California in 1969 and 1970 and with Lelah Vegas Gass Slaughter at Pacifica, California in 1970. Original recordings are in the possession of the author. Florence Lee Jones Cahlan interviewed Lelah Slaughter at Ontario, California in a series of ten interviews in 1955. Transcripts of these, amounting to about seventy legal-size pages, afford the most significant source of information about Gass. Dennis Casebier interviewed Fenton Gass in 1967 and prepared a transcript. The above documents will surely be recognized as the outstanding primary source material on Las Vegas Ranch and O. D. Gass, for none of his children survive.

Gass left only three daybooks of Las Vegas Ranch and virtually no personal papers. All are in private possession. The daybooks were photo copied and are in the author's file.

Dennis Casebier's excellent monograph, *Camp El Dorado, Arizona Territory* (1970) explains the military situation at Las Vegas Ranch in the late 1860's. Also helpful were census records for 1870 and 1880, obtained from the National Archives. Census lists of Arizona Territory in 1864 and Nevada State in 1875 also were consulted. Voting records of San Bernardino County, California, helped establish Gass' residences in later years. Books of deeds, voting registers and county commissioners' minutes of Lincoln County, Nevada, on file at Pioche, provided a wealth of information.

Other references about Gass and his ranch appear in a number of places. Some of these are: H. H. Bancroft, *History of Arizona and New Mexico* (1889); *Appendix to Nevada State Senate Journal*, "Nevada State Mineralogist's Report for 1871-72", Journal of George M. Wheeler, *U. S. Geographical Surveys West of the 100th Meridian* (1871), and Helen Gibbon's *Saint and Savage* (1965). Dennis Casebier's military research into the "Letter Book of the District of Upper Colorado, Camp Mohave, A. T."

uncovered personal mentions about Gass not available elsewhere.

Newspaper research frequently results in uncovering unexpected information. Regular mention of Gass was in the Prescott *Arizona Miner* and the *Daily Arizona Miner*, during 1866-1871, while less frequently his name appeared in the Los Angeles *Star* from the mid-1850's to the early 1860's and in the Pioche *Record* in the 1870's and early 1880's. Useful items also came from the *Mining and Scientific Press*, the San Francisco *Alta*, the *Arizona Citizen* in Tucson, the *Daily Telegraph* in Salt Lake City, *Our Dixie Times* published in St. George, Utah, the *Arizona Weekly Enterprise* in Florence, Arizona and the Yuma *Republican*.

Pah-Ute County always has been an interesting political entity for scholars and history buffs alike. James H. McClintock's *Mormon Settlement in Arizona* has interesting data, but the best and most complete treatment of that entity is Don Bufkin's "The Lost County of Pah-Ute", *Arizoniana* (issue No. 2, 1964). Additional information about Pah-Ute County and other southern Nevada boundary problems is in the *Political History of Nevada* (1965), issued by the Secretary of the State of Nevada. Arthur Palmer did the research.

CHAPTER FIVE. The founding of Las Vegas was written after extensive reading of Southwestern newspapers. The Las Vegas *Age*, *Lincoln County Record* in Pioche, and the Los Angeles *Times* were read by the volume. Other important newspapers were the Los Angeles *Examiner*, Searchlight (Nevada) *Bulletin*, Delamar (Nevada) *Lode*, and Salt Lake City *Tribune*.

Spicy interviews with teamster Ray Gibson of Laguna Beach, California, provided much color, as did a reading of the memoirs of Charles "Pop" Squires, on file at the University of Nevada, Las Vegas. David Myrick's *Railroads of Nevada and Eastern California, Volume Two* (1963) furnished thorough coverage of early twentieth century Southern Nevada railroad building.

CHAPTER SIX. The files of newspapers mentioned above relating to Chapter Five also were used to write about the creation of Clark County. Interviews with Henry H. Lee were especially helpful. Other detail was obtained by research in courthouse records in both Lincoln and Clark Counties. The *Statutes of the State of Nevada* also were consulted.

CHAPTER SEVEN. The short history of Las Vegas' later years was compiled after reading numerous issues of the Las Vegas *Age* and the Las Vegas *Re-*

view, later the *Evening Review-Journal*. That newspaper's Golden Anniversary Progress Edition published in March 1955 and compiled by Florence Lee Jones Cahlan gives annual summaries of Las Vegas history from 1905 until the mid-1930's, when Hoover (Boulder) Dam was completed. Also in that same edition are sections devoted to the development of local transportation, various businesses, institutions, entertainment and nearby cities.

One large picture-filled chapter of David Myrick's book (mentioned above) gives the most thorough coverage of Hoover Dam construction of any book now in print.

Trusted information about Las Vegas after the Hoover Dam era is in *Sagebrush Casinos* (1953) written by Oscar Lewis and in Richard Lillard's highly readable *Desert Challenge* (1942). Hillyer and Best's *Las Vegas Playtown U.S.A.* offers good depth of the freewheeling Las Vegas life previous to its publication in 1955. Conversations and interviews with long-time Las Vegas residents (many of whom are listed in the acknowledgments section) also contributed to the development of this chapter.

Picture Credits

The lower case "a" denotes picture on the top of a page; "b" and "c" are those in descending order. Numerals in parentheses designate quantity of pictures on the page.

California State Library, 77, 78.

Clark County Wholesale Mercantile Company (courtesy of Lorin Ronnow), 114b, 116, 122, 123(2).

Church of Jesus Christ of Latter-Day Saints, Historian's Office, 20, 21, 26, 27, 28, 29.

Garehime Music Company, 138, 143a.

Sherwin "Scoop" Garside, 85b, 93c, 137b, 140(2), 142b, 143b, 144b, 146a, 148(2), 149b, 151, 152(2), 153 a and c, 154, 155a, 156(2), 157(2), 158(2), 159(2), 160(2), 161, 162b, 163a, 168a. Many of these pictures were taken by Las Vegas photographers M. M. Oakes and Glenn Davis.

Fenton Gass, 38, 47, 48, 49, 50.

Captain Ray Gibson, 94.

Mazie Martin Jones, 129a, 141b.

Las Vegas City Library, 107, 118a, 125b.

Las Vegas News Bureau, 100b.

Las Vegas *Review-Journal* (courtesy of Bill Vincent), 110, 132b, 147b.

Henry H. Lee, 109.

O. Dock Marston, 41.

National Park Service (courtesy of Pete Sanchez, Death Valley), 86c, 102a.

Gerald "Butch" Nelson, 112a, 117a, 131a, 132a, 133.

Pomona Public Library, 111, 169b.

Sal Sagev Hotel (courtesy of Carolyn Miller), 128b.

Dennis Schieck photo, 170(2), 171(4).

Florin Slaughter, 54, 56.

The Stay Family (courtesy of John McNamee), 44(2), 58a, 59a, 66, 67(2), 68, 75a, 84b, 88, 89(2), 92b, 97, 98, 100a, 103, 126b, 127, 129b, 130a. These pictures were collected by pioneer Las Vegan Helen J. Stewart.

Fred Steen, 106.

Union Pacific Railroad Company (courtesy of Allen Krieg), 70, 145a, 146b.

University of Nevada Las Vegas Library, Special Collections (courtesy of Stephen Powell), 45(2), 59b, 69b, 75b, 76, 82, 85a, 86b, 90a, 92a, 93a, 96, 98b, 99, 108, 112b, 118b, 128a, 136, 141a, 142a, 144a, 145b, 150, 165(2), 166(4), 167. Most of these pictures are from the albums of W. E. Ferron, Leon Rockwell and Walter Bracken, on deposit there.

Ed Von Tobel Lumber Company (courtesy of Jake Von Tobel and Ed Von Tobel, Jr.), 72(2), 73(2), 82a, 90c, 114a, 124a, 125c, 130c.

Buster Wilson, 62.

Mrs. Maureen H. Wilson, 58b, 60, 61(3), 84a, 86a, 90b, 93b, 101(2), 104b, 119, 130b, 132c, 134, 135, 137a, 139(2), 147a, 153b, 162a. These pictures are among the historical materials amassed by her late husband Fred Wilson.

John Yount, 63(3).

Roy E. Purcell artwork appears on pages 10, 13, 15, 18, 36, 39, 40, 52, 64, 80.

The Bank of Nevada, courtesy of Charles Siefert, furnished the paintings on pages 17 and 24. They are original artwork by Merv Corning of Los Angeles.

The Dellenbaugh painting which appears on page 42 is used by permission of its owner, Clifford A. Jones.

† indicates map reference.
Bold face indicates picture reference.

181

Other Books by Nevada Publications

P.O. Box 15444, Las Vegas, Nevada 89114

AN EDITOR ON THE COMSTOCK LODE, by Wells Drury. 343 pages, illus. These reminiscences of Comstock society comprise a vivid cross-section of life. Author portrays the bad men, the law and various personalities as he found them.

MINING CAMP DAYS by Emil W. Billeb. 229 pages, illus. The author provides insights into Nevada and eastern California mining camps after 1905. Dozens of unpublished photographs were taken by this observer-participant, augmenting a good text.

MARK TWAIN, YOUNG REPORTER IN VIRGINIA CITY, by Katharine Hillyer. 92 pages, illus. Informal collection of Twain episodes at the *Territorial Enterprise*.

SILVER KINGS: THE LIVES AND TIMES OF MACKAY, FAIR, FLOOD, AND O'BRIEN, by Oscar Lewis. 286 pages, illus. The story of the Comstock Lode is retold with short biographies of these four men who controlled the richest strike in North America.

PLACER GOLD DEPOSITS IN NEVADA, by M.C. Johnson. (USGS Bull. 1356) 118 pages. County by county summary of 115 Nevada placer districts. Locations, extent of deposits and history.

THE MAKING OF A HARDROCK MINER, by Stephen Voynick. 224 pages, illus. Intimate description of life working underground—the heat, water, dark, constant danger. Much human interest.

VIRGINIA & TRUCKEE, A STORY OF VIRGINIA CITY AND THE COMSTOCK TIMES, by Lucius Beebe, 63 pages, illus., maps, biblio., tables. Few short lines were as familiar to powerful interests and celebrated to the world as the glorious V&T. This fast-moving account describes the mines that furnished ore for the silver mills along the Carson River. After 79 years the rails were ripped up in 1938.

NEVADA PLACE NAMES, by Helen Carlson. 280 pages. Treasure-trove of facts about the origins of names in Nevada's towns, natural features.

THE TOWN THAT DIED LAUGHING, by Oscar Lewis. 235 pages. The story of Austin, a rambunctious early day Nevada mining camp, and of its newspaper, The Reese River Reveille.

THE COMPLEAT NEVADA TRAVELER, by David W. toll. 192 pages, illus. The author divides Nevada into five regions in order to describe in each of them its history, services for travelers, annual events and assorted trivia. Interesting photographs (some in color) are interspersed amid a lively text.

THE NEWSPAPERS OF NEVADA, by Richard Lingenfelter. 336 pages, illus., index. History of 800 publications issued from various Nevada localities. A thorough study.

TOURING NEVADA: A HISTORIC AND SCENIC GUIDE, by Mary Ellen and Al Glass. 253 pages, illus. Nevada travel descriptions for visitor and resident alike. Maps and color index are definite aids. Color cover.

THE STORY OF CANDELARIA AND ITS NEIGHBORS: COLUMBUS, METALLIC CITY, BELLEVILLE, MARIETTA, SODAVILLE AND COALDALE, by Hugh Shamberger. 200 pages, illus. History of mining in southwestern Nevada; an important study.

COPPER TIMES, by Jack Fleming. 255 pages, Collection of stories on Whte Pine County—its people, towns, copper industry, recreation, education, history.

EUREKA AND ITS RESOURCES, by Lambert Molinelli. 136 pages, illus. Good, short history of the mines, issued in 1879.

RAWHIDE, by Hugh A. Shamberger. 50 pages, maps. Early history, development, and water supply of this mining camp in Mineral County.

A MINER'S CHRISTMAS CAROL, AND OTHER FRONTIER TALES, by Sam Davis. 86 pages. A turn-of-the-century Carson City editor writes of early Pioche, Carson City, Virginia City, and newspapering.

RAILROADS OF NEVADA AND EASTERN CALIFORNIA, VOL. 1, by David F. Myrick. 451 pages, illus, maps. Author details 43 Nevada lines, from the Central Pacific to those serving Tonopah-Goldfield-Ely booms. Numerous illustrations augment the definitive text which also includes politics, social life, and Nevada personalities.

DEEP ENOUGH, by Frank Crampton. 281 pages, True-to-life autobiography of a working stiff in the Nevada mining camps.

INDIANS OF COO-YE-EE PAH, by Nellie Harner. 145 pages. History of Northern Paiutes from a native's point of view.

REPORT OF THE EXPLORATIONS ACROSS THE GREAT BASIN IN 1859 FOR A DIRECT WAGON-ROUTE TO GENOA, by James Simpson. 518 pages, illus. Author moved westward across central Nevada in 1858, noting the plants, animals, birds, Indians, etc.

GOLDFIELD, by Hugh A. Shamberger. 240 pages, illus. The early history, the mines, the struggle for water, the building of railroads and the Gans-Nelson fight of 1906—are described. Author details rise of corporate mining and highgrading.

GEOLOGY OF THE GREAT BASIN, by Bill Fiero. 250 pages, illus. A fine treatment complete with maps charts and analysis of Nevada geology. Author covers basic geologic conceptes and processes and complex geologic history. Striking color photographs augment the text.

CAMELS IN NEVADA, by Douglas McDonald. 32 pages, illus. In Nevada camel pack trains hauled salt, wood and even freight, also aiding early surveyors. But the beasts also brought problems. Modern camel races in Virginia City are recounted.

SAND IN A WHIRLWIND, THE PAIUTE INDIAN WAR OF 1860, by Ferol Egan. 316 pages, illus. The author tells the familiar story of the Pyramid Lake War of 1860, with the narrative presented in fictional dialogue.

SURVIVAL ARTS OF THE PRIMITIVE PAIUTES, by Margaret Wheat. 117 pages, illus. Author documents the feeding and clothing making techniques of northern Paiutes.

HIGHGRADE, THE MINING STORY OF NATIONAL, NEVADA, by Nancy B. Shreier. 150 pages, illus. Detailed account of the rich National district north of Winnemucca, during 1907-13.

TREBLE V, THE LEGACY OF A CATTLE BARON OF THE OLD WEST, by R. Guild Gray. 668 pages. Well written story of several generations of Nevada trappers, ranch-

---

For a complete catalog of our books write to:

Nevada Publications • Box 15444 • Las Vegas, Nevada 89114